The Tyndale New Testament Commentaries

General Editor: Professor R. V. G. Tasker, M.A., D.D.

THE GENERAL EPISTLE OF JAMES

THE GENERAL EPISTLE OF

JAMES

AN INTRODUCTION AND COMMENTARY

by

R. V. G. TASKER, M.A., D.D.

Professor Emeritus of New Testament Exegesis
in the University of London

INTER-VARSITY PRESS

Universities and Colleges Christian Fellowship
39 Bedford Square, London WC1B 3EY

First Edition–November 1957
Reprinted 1961, 1964,
1967, 1969, 1973, 1974

HARDBACK EDITION 0 85111 600 0
PAPERBACK EDITION 0 85111 805 4

Made and printed in England by
STAPLES PRINTERS LIMITED
at The Stanhope Press, Rochester Kent.

GENERAL PREFACE

ALL who are interested in the teaching and the study of the New Testament today cannot fail to be concerned with the lack of commentaries which avoid the extremes of being unduly technical or unhelpfully brief. It is the hope of the editor and publishers that this present series will do something towards the supply of this deficiency. Their aim is to place in the hands of students and serious readers of the New Testament, at a moderate cost, commentaries by a number of scholars who, while they are free to make their own individual contributions, are united in a common desire to promote a truly biblical theology.

The commentaries are primarily exegetical and only secondarily homiletic, though it is hoped that both student and preacher will find them informative and suggestive. Critical questions are fully considered in introductory sections, and also, at the author's discretion, in additional notes.

The commentaries are based on the Authorized Version, partly because this is the version which most Bible readers possess, and partly because it is easier for commentators, working on this foundation, to show why, on textual and linguistic grounds, the later versions are so often to be preferred. No one translation is regarded as infallible, and no single Greek manuscript or group of manuscripts is regarded as always right! Greek words are transliterated to help those unfamiliar with the language and to save those who do know Greek the trouble of discovering what word is being discussed.

There are many signs today of a renewed interest in what the Bible has to say and of a more general desire to understand its meaning as fully and clearly as possible. It is the hope of all those concerned with this series that God will graciously use what they have written to further this end.

R. V. G. Tasker.

CHIEF ABBREVIATIONS

A.V.	English Authorized Version (King James).
R.V.	English Revised Version, 1881.
R.S.V.	American Revised Standard Version, 1946.
Calvin	Commentary on James in *Commentaries on the Catholic Epistles*, translated by John Owen, 1855.
Hort	*The Epistle of St. James* (The Greek Text with commentary, as far as iv. 7), 1909.
Knowling	*The Epistle of St. James*, R. J. Knowling, 1904.
Mayor	*The Epistle of St. James*, J. B. Mayor, Third Edition, 1913.
Ropes	*A Critical and Exegetical Commentary on the Epistle of St. James*, J. H. Ropes (*International Critical Commentary*), 1916.
Tyndale	*The New Testament, 1534*, William Tyndale (C.U.P., 1938).

ACKNOWLEDGEMENTS

Permission to quote from the R.S.V. has been kindly given by the copyright owners, The National Council of the Churches of Christ in the United States of America.

CONTENTS

FATHER IN HEAVEN,
what is man that Thou visitest him, and the son of man that Thou art mindful of him? Verily, Thou dost never leave Thyself without a witness; and at last Thou didst give to man Thy Word. More Thou couldst not do; to compel him to make use of it, to hear it and read it, to compel him to act according to it, Thou couldst not wish. And yet Thou didst do more. For Thou art not like a man. Rarely does he do any thing for nothing, and if he does, he at least would not be put to inconvenience by it. Thou, on the contrary, O God, bestowest Thy Word as a gift,—and we men have nothing to give in return. And if only Thou dost find some willingness on the part of a single individual, Thou art prompt to help, and, with divine patience, dost sit and spell it out with him that he may be able rightly to understand it; and, again with divine patience, Thou dost take him as it were by the hand and help him when he strives to act accordingly,—Thou our Father in heaven.

From a prayer by
SOREN KIERKEGAARD.

AUTHOR'S PREFACE

MY interest in the Epistle of James dates from a sermon heard as a boy in my school chapel. I have retained a vivid recollection of the preacher, a distinguished headmaster of a rival school who was destined to become an equally distinguished dignitary of the Church; and I have never forgotten the text, 'Pure religion and undefiled before God and the Father is this, To visit the fatherless and widows in their affliction, and to keep himself unspotted from the world'. It may have been that the recent death of my father impressed the words with special vividness upon my memory; though it is surely one of the most unforgettable texts of Scripture. One brief sentence in the sermon itself has also remained uppermost in my mind. 'The Epistle of James is a collection of sermon-notes.' However inadequate this may be as a description of the Epistle, it is suggestive, and contains more than a modicum of truth. For almost every sentence of this eloquent and challenging document, with its vivid and arresting images, its aphorisms and its paradoxes, its irony and its scorn, calls for further exposition and elucidation: and the preacher who has himself been inspired by it, could scarcely fail to impart something of that inspiration to others.

Be this as it may, it is my belief that the message of the Epistle is vital for Christian evangelism. That must be my excuse, if excuse is needed, should any reader feel that at certain places in this commentary the needs of the preacher have been more fully met than those of the enquiring student. I am, however, confident that such a student will in fact find here, within the necessarily limited space at my disposal, the material he requires for an intelligent understanding of this by no means easy letter. 'St. James', R. A. Knox has said, 'is always full of difficulties when he looks deceptively simple. The difficulty is not so much understanding what he said as in understanding why he said it.'[1] Connections between different parts of the Epistle are indeed not easy to establish; and it would seem that we are dealing, as the preacher in the school chapel suggested, not with one sermon but with the seed-bed of many sermons. Certainly a Christian commentator on this Epistle needs to be especially careful not to divorce scholarship from religion, theology from preaching, and the wisdom of the head from the wisdom of the heart.

It is probably true to say that this letter is not valued as highly as it ought to be. Catholics have been too content just to find in it Scriptural authority for what they call the sacrament of extreme unction, or else to use it as a stick with which to attack the hated doctrine of *justificatio fide sola*. Protestants, on the other hand, are still consciously or unconsciously influenced by Luther's devaluation of the Epistle, and tend to feel that, in spite of its presence in the New Testament, it is somewhat sub-Christian. My endeavour in this commentary has been to consider it within its Christian context as an essential part of the collection of writings which constitutes the canon of Scripture.

As part of the New Testament, the Epistle has a permanent message both for the Church as a whole and for each individual Christian. There would, however, seem to be special times, both in the history of the Church and in the spiritual pilgrimage of the believer, when its message sounds forth with special relevance. Whenever faith does not issue in love, and dogma, however orthodox, is unrelated to life; whenever Christians are tempted to settle down to a self-centred religion, and become oblivious of the social and material needs of others; or whenever they deny by their manner of living the creed they profess, and seem more anxious to be friends of the world than friends of God, then the Epistle of James has something to say to them which they disregard at their peril. It is surely both interesting and illuminating to recall that, when Soren Kierkegaard in the middle of the nineteenth century felt called to use his great gifts of eloquence and satire in a sustained warfare

[1] *The Epistles and Gospels*, Burns Oates and Washbourne, 1946, pp. 137, 133.

against the worldliness and hypocrisy of the contemporary Church, it was the Epistle of James that both inspired him for the battle and supplied him with the ammunition with which to fight. 'Kierkegaard, while acknowledging the truth of Justification by Faith, as directed against "work-righteousness" and the assumption that one can earn his righteousness, had seen that the temper of the times "especially in Protestantism, and more especially in Denmark" required the proclamation of a complementary truth—a bringing to the fore of the practical, ethical side of Christianity, not by any means to the exclusion or minimizing of its dogmatic aspect, but to the exclusion of that barren orthodoxy which would make mere intellectual belief the primary act of Christian faith. The highly practical Epistle of James . . . was and remained Kierkegaard's favourite Scripture.'[1] He has left behind him some remarkable discourses on it, particularly those on the subjects 'The Mirror of the Word' (i. 22–27); 'The Unchangeableness of God' (i. 17–21); and 'Purity of heart is to will one thing' (iv. 8).

This Epistle would seem to be of especial value to the individual Christian during what we might describe as the second stage in his pilgrim's progress. After he has been led to respond to the gospel of grace, and come to have the joyful assurance that he is a redeemed child of God, if he is to advance along the way of holiness, and if the ethical implications of his new faith are to be translated into practical realities, then he needs the stimulus and the challenge of the Epistle of James. As there are many in our land today who are in this precise position, it may well be that few books are more relevant to the contemporary situation.

Many English-speaking scholars have given prolonged study to the elucidation of the Epistle; and no one can write about it without being continually in their debt. The great commentaries of J. B. Mayor and J. H. Ropes, both monuments of learning, and the unfinished posthumous work of F. J. A. Hort have been constantly at my side. Though they vary much in their understanding of the Epistle, and though their conclu-

[1] *A Kierkegaard Anthology*, Robert Brettall, O.U.P., 1947, p. 282.

ions are not always acceptable, their work is of lasting value. I have also seldom failed to see what that master-commentator John Calvon has to say, for he understood this Epistle so much better than Martin Luther, and had the great gift of seeing the New Testament 'steadily and seeing it whole'.

INTRODUCTION

THE PLACE OF THE EPISTLE IN THE NEW TESTAMENT

THE Epistle of James is found in our English Bibles after the Epistle to the Hebrews as the first of the seven Epistles known as the 'General' or 'Catholic' Epistles. The Church historian Eusebius (b. 265) was the first to describe these letters in this way. Previously Clement of Alexandria had referred to the letter sent out by the Apostolic Council at Jerusalem (see Acts xv) as a 'catholic epistle', and Origen (b. 185) had described the Epistle of Barnabas and the Epistles of John, Peter and Jude in the same manner. The meaning of the expression is given in the preface to an anonymous commentary on the Epistle of James ascribed to Oecumenius, a Bishop in Thessaly, about the year 600. There we read, 'These Epistles are said to be catholic because they are encyclical. For this company of the Lord's disciples did not address their letters, as the inspired Paul addressed his Epistles to the Romans and Corinthians, separately to one nation or city, but collectively to those who were believers.' As the second and third Epistles of John, though addressed to individuals, were regarded as appendages to the First Epistle, this definition can be applied to this whole group of documents without reserve.

It is only, however, since the publication of the Great Bible in 1539 that James has occupied this particular place in the English Bible. That was the first occasion when the order of books in English translations was made to conform to that of the Latin Vulgate. Hitherto, English editors had been in this matter under the influence of Luther. He had arbitrarily, and without any support from ancient MSS., placed the four books which he considered to be of doubtful apostolic authority and of secondary value doctrinally at the end of his New Testament published in 1522, to form a kind of supplement; and he did not number them in the table of contents. These books were Hebrews, James, Jude and Revelation. In the introduction to that edition, Luther wrote the following important and often-quoted words which are here given in Ropes' translation.

'In fine, Saint John's Gospel and his first Epistle, Saint Paul's Epistles, especially those to the Romans, Galatians, Ephesians, and Saint Peter's first Epistle,—these are the books which show thee Christ, and teach thee everything that is needful and blessed for thee to know even though thou never see or hear any other book or doctrine. Therefore is Saint James's Epistle a right strawy Epistle in comparison with them, for it has no gospel character to it.'

Luther was no doubt under the influence of the stylistic criticisms of the Epistle made by Erasmus in 1516, that it lacked *maiestatem illam et gravitatem apostolicam*, and that the language was not so Hebraic as would naturally be expected in a bishop of Jerusalem. But it would also seem certain that Luther was prejudiced against the Epistle by the use that was made of it by the Papists in defence of the doctrine of justification by works and of the sacrament of extreme unction. As the expression 'right strawy Epistle' (suggested by 1 Cor. iii. 12) is often quoted in isolation, it is well to notice the following words *in comparison with them*. Luther did not reject James as being all straw, for in the special preface to the Epistle he wrote that, in spite of its teaching about justification by works which, as will be shown in this commentary, he misunderstood, he nevertheless valued the Epistle. 'I will not have it in my Bible in the number of the proper chief books', he said, 'but do not intend thereby to forbid anyone to place and exalt it as he pleases, for there is many a good saying in it.'

Tyndale in his translations of the New Testament (1525 and 1534) followed Luther's order, and also gave no numbering to these four 'secondary' books in the table of contents. In his prologue to James he also repeats some of the strictures of Luther; but on the whole his verdict, here given in modern English, is more favourable.

'Though this Epistle was rejected in old time and not considered by many to be the Epistle of a true apostle, and though also it does not lay the foundation of the faith of Christ, but speaks of a general faith in God, neither preaching His death and resurrection, nor the mercy that is laid up in store for us in Him, nor the everlasting covenant made for us by His blood, which is the office and duty of a true apostle, as Christ says "You shall testify of Me": yet, because it sets up no human doctrine, but calls upon men to keep the law of God, and makes love which is without partiality the fulfilling of the law, as Christ and all the apostles did, and has in reference to this many good and Godly sentences in it; and has also nothing that is not agreeable to the rest of the Scriptures, if it be considered impartially, I think it ought rightly to be regarded as Holy Scripture.'

Tyndale clearly saw, as did Calvin later, that there is no contradiction between Paul and James on the question of justification by faith and works. In his commentary on the Catholic Epistles published in 1551 Calvin, though he retained the Lutheran order of the books, reminded his readers in the foreword to the commentary on James that 'though James seems more sparing in proclaiming the grace of Christ than it behoved an apostle to be, it is not surely required of all to handle the same arguments'. And his conclusion is: 'It is enough to make men receive this Epistle, that it contains nothing unworthy of an apostle of Christ. It is indeed full of instruction on various subjects, the benefit of which extends to every part of the Christian life; for there are here remarkable passages on patience, prayer to God, the excellency and fruit of heavenly truth, humility, holy duties, the restraining of the tongue, the cultivation of peace, the repression of lusts, the contempt of the world, and the like.'

The order in which the seven Catholic Epistles are found in A.V. and R.V., viz. James, 1 and 2 Peter, 1, 2 and 3 John, Jude, is, as has already been mentioned, the order of the Latin Vulgate. It is also the order of almost all Greek MSS. and most of the ancient lists of books found in Patristic writings. It would seem to owe its origin to the order in which the three 'pillars' of the Church, James, Cephas and John, are mentioned in Gal. ii. 9. The main variant to this order is that which places the Petrine Epistles first, and the Johannine Epistles second, followed by James and Jude.[1] This latter order, found in Augustine, Rufinus, the Apostolic Constitutions, and the list of books drawn up at the Council of Carthage in 397, reflects the growing authority in the fourth and fifth centuries of the see of Rome, and hence of Peter its alleged founder. In the east, priority was given to James, which is described by Eusebius as 'the first of the Epistles styled catholic'.

But, while the order of the seven Catholic Epistles varied very little, the position in the New Testament of the collection as a whole varied rather more. It was often the practice to place these Epistles along with the Acts of the Apostles in a codex by themselves, distinguishing them from other codices which might contain only the four Gospels, or only the Pauline Epistles. Such codices containing Acts plus the Catholic Epistles are known as *Praxapostoloi*; and, very naturally, when complete editions of the New Testament were constructed which made use of these *Praxapostoloi*, the Catholic Epistles would be inserted after Acts, either before or after the Pauline Epistles. Thus in the Complutensian Polyglot, the first Greek Testament to be printed,[2] though not the first to be published, the order of the New Testament books is the Four Gospels, the Pauline Epistles, Acts followed by the Catholic Epistles, and the Apocalypse. This order is found in no other extant ancient authority except the famous Codex Sinaiticus found by Tischendorf on Mount Sinai and now in the British Museum. In the other great fourth-century codex, the Codex Vaticanus, Acts and the Catholic Epistles precede the Pauline letters. It was usual, however, to regard Acts as an introduction to the whole of the New Testament epistolary, and to place the Catholic Epistles by themselves after the Pauline collection, as in the Latin Vulgate and the English Bibles.

This somewhat secondary position finally assigned to the

[1] A 'canon' or list of books of unknown date found in Codex Claromontanus, a Graeco-Latin MS. of the Pauline Epistles written in the sixth century, probably in Sardinia, has the order 1 and 2 Peter, James, 1, 2, 3 John, Jude.

[2] Though it was completed on 10th January, 1514, publication was delayed till 1522. Meanwhile Erasmus' edition had been published at Basle in 1516.

Catholic Epistles seemed in harmony with the doubts that had been expressed in the Early Church about the apostolicity of the lesser members of this group. 1 Peter and 1 John had in fact alone received general recognition from the earliest days; and they are the only Catholic Epistles which satisfy the criterion of canonicity laid down in Article VI of the Thirty-nine Articles, 'books of whose authority there was never any doubt in the Church'. About all the others there was considerable hesitation before they had an assured place in the New Testament canon.

Although the Epistle of James had become firmly established in the canon of the western part of Christendom by the end of the fourth century, it is interesting to notice that the tenth-century Codex Corbeiensis[1] (referred to in the subsequent commentary as 'the Corbey MS.'), whose text reflects that of an old Latin translation of this Epistle made in the fourth century, contains James, the Epistle of Barnabas and two comparatively unimportant patristic works, but no other Biblical book. This unique phenomenon suggests that, even at this comparatively late date, in the west, the Epistle may not have been very highly regarded. Moreover, the somewhat erratic translation found in this codex, representing, as we have seen, a pre-Vulgate text, supports Augustine's complaint that the Epistle of James had been very badly translated into Latin. The Epistle is absent from the list of books in the Muratorian fragment, which reflects the attitude of the Roman church to the canon of Scripture at the end of the second century, and also from a list giving the position of the African church in 360, which was discovered in 1885 by Theodor Mommsen in a MS. at Cheltenham and is sometimes known as 'the Cheltenham list'. It becomes fully established as a canonical book in the west after its inclusion by Jerome in the Latin Vulgate about 385. Jerome, however, was not without doubts about its authenticity, for he wrote, 'James who is called the Lord's brother wrote one Epistle only, which is one of the seven catholic Epistles, which, it is asserted, was published under his

[1] Originally found in the Benedictine monastery at Corbie near Amiens and now in Leningrad.

name by another, although little by little as time went on it obtained authority'.

In the Greek-speaking church, the first clear reference to the Epistle as Scripture and as the work of James is found in Origen. In commenting on Jn. viii. 24, in the portion of his Commentary on John written after his removal from Alexandria to Caesarea in 231, he states that even if a man who is dead in his sins says he believes Christ, he does not truly believe Him. He then adds: 'If faith is spoken of, but is without works, such faith is dead as we read in the current Epistle of James.' Elsewhere he introduces references to the Epistle with words implying canonicity, such as 'James writes', 'the apostle says', 'it stands written'. It is also probable that Origen's predecessor at the catechetical school at Alexandria, Clement, was familiar with the Epistle; for, although there are no references to it in Clement's extant works, Eusebius remarks, 'Clement has given us abridged accounts of all the canonical Scriptures, not even omitting those that are disputed. I mean the book of Jude and the other Catholic Epistles.' Some scholars have thought it probable that there are references to James in the apostolic Fathers of the second century, but this must remain uncertain.[1] Through the influence of Origen, the Epistle was accepted at Alexandria and found a place in the Egyptian versions. Eusebius, the best part of a century later, classes James among the 'disputed books which are nevertheless familiar to most writers'; and in another place, speaking more in detail about it, he says, 'The first of the Epistles styled Catholic is said to be by James the Lord's brother; but it ought to be known that it is held by some to be spurious. Certainly not many ancient writers have mentioned it.' He himself seems to regard the Epistle as canonical and makes quotations from it.

When we turn to the Syrian church we find that no translation from the Greek into Syriac was made till the Peshitto or Syriac Vulgate version of 412, which included the three major Catholic Epistles, James, 1 Peter and 1 John. We also find that

[1] The relevant passages are cited in full in the Introduction to Mayor; but Mayor's inferences from the evidence have not been generally accepted by scholars.

some Greek-speaking members of the Syrian church did not recognize James as part of the New Testament. Theodore of Mopsuestia, for example, who died in 429, accepted none of the Catholic Epistles. It was pressure from the Western Syrians associated with the churches of Antioch and Edessa that led gradually to the general acceptance of all these Epistles in the more distant parts of eastern Christendom in the sixth and seventh centuries.

It would seem that the chief reason for the lack of quotations from the Epistle in early Christian writers, and for the hesitation that was felt in many quarters about accepting its authenticity, was uncertainty about the identification of the 'James' mentioned as the author in the opening verse. As long as this remained in doubt there would always be some who, as Eusebius says, held it to be a spurious work; or, as Jerome put it, a letter published by someone else under the apostle's name. But when it became more generally recognized that the author was James the brother of the Lord, described as an apostle by Paul (Gal. i. 19), the way was open for a more universal acceptance of its authority. There does not seem any patristic evidence to lead us to suppose that the problem which troubled Luther, the apparent contradiction between James and Paul on the question of justification, was a primary cause for the delay in including the work among the canonical books of the New Testament.

We should probably do well to remember in this connection that the Early Church was primarily a missionary church, and that letters to the young churches written by their own missionaries, which dealt specifically with the fundamental doctrines of their faith and with the particular social and moral problems with which they were confronted, would inevitably be more often copied and more widely circulated than a 'general' Epistle such as the Epistle of James. Its author might indeed speak with authority and be addressing a wide audience on important matters, but that authority could never be quite the same as that of the apostles who had first spoken to them the gospel of God.

THE AUTHORSHIP OF THE EPISTLE

As we have seen from the evidence of Eusebius and Jerome, there were some in the Early Church who regarded the Epistle of James as pseudepigraphic. This view has also commended itself to those modern scholars, who on general considerations assign it a late date, and who regard it as a moral treatise rather than a letter. It was by this means, they suppose, that the work of a later writer was given some kind of apostolic authority. Thus Martin Dibelius writes: 'It is comprehensible that a Christian at the end of the first century who wished to impress a practical Christianity upon the Church would choose James as his patron since he was called "the righteous".'[1] The tendency of such critics is either to assume that the author himself added the first verse, the only strictly epistolary feature of the document, in which case the Epistle was pseudepigraphic from the very beginning; or else to suppose that this verse was a later addition of the Early Church to what was originally a completely anonymous writing. The decisive argument against both these suppositions would seem to be the lack of any emphasis upon the apostle's personality and activities.[2] The advocates of a pseudepigraphic origin of all or some of the Catholic Epistles cannot have it both ways. If the Second Epistle of Peter is regarded by them as pseudepigraphic largely because the writer describes himself as 'an apostle of Jesus Christ' and because it contains several references of an autobiographical character, it is strange that the Epistle of James is regarded as pseudepigraphic in spite of the absence of any reference to the author's being an apostle and an entire lack of any personal details about him. If the criteria of pseudepigraphy are so uncertain, we seem to be on surer ground if we assume that, even in the case of books which were received into the canon of the New Testament comparatively late, there was general agreement that they really were the works of the author whose names they bear, even if, as in the case of James, their identity was difficult to establish.

[1] *Fresh approach to the New Testament and early Christian literature*, p. 230.
[2] *Introduction to the Literature of the New Testament*, J. Moffatt, T. and T. Clark, third edition, 1918, p. 472.

If this Epistle is not pseudepigraphic, we are left with the problem of the identification of the James who describes himself as 'a servant of God and of the Lord Jesus Christ'. It may be that he is a person about whom nothing else is known, as the name was a common one; but it is improbable that a writer, otherwise entirely unknown, would have composed such an authoritative exhortation, and addressed it, apparently, to Christendom as a whole (see the commentary on i. 1). Moreover, if this is the correct explanation of the authorship, we are forced to the unsatisfactory conclusion that the Epistle came to be regarded as the work of James the apostle, when in reality it was written by someone with no apostolic authority whatever. Nevertheless, this solution of the problem proved acceptable to Erasmus and also to Luther, who ascribed the letter to 'some good, pious man who had taken some sayings from the apostle's disciples'.[1]

The tradition that became established in the Church that the Epistle was not only apostolic but should be attributed to James, the head of the Early Church at Jerusalem, has most claims to be accepted as true. Not only is it incapable of being scientifically disproved, but it has much intrinsic probability. The fact that the Epistle has seldom been regarded as the work of one of the original twelve apostles affords it some negative support. There is very little evidence, for example, that the author was considered to be James the son of Zebedee. The Corbey MS. of the tenth century has a subscription to the Epistle *Explicit epistola Iacobi filii Zaebedei.* Moreover, a series of Spanish writers from the seventh to the seventeenth centuries were, in Ropes' words, 'led by national patriotism to claim the Epistle for their apostle and patron St. James'. The decisions reached at the Council of Trent 1546 did not, in deference to Spanish Catholics, rule out the possibility of the authorship of the son of Zebedee, but merely insisted that the Epistle was the work of 'the apostle James'. This comprises all the evidence from Catholic sources. No Protestant scholar has taken this view of the authorship seriously, for the very good reason that James the son of Zebedee was martyred by Herod Agrippa I

[1] Quoted by Ropes, p. 45.

in the year 44 (see Acts xii. 2); and it is almost impossible to date the Epistle as early as his authorship would demand.

The other member of the original apostolic band bearing the same name is James, the son of Alphaeus and Mary, who was distinguished from the other James by the nickname 'the little one' (see Mk. iii. 18, xv. 40). There is, however, no evidence that the Epistle was ever assigned to him in the Early Church. The possibility of his authorship was nevertheless not ruled out by some of the Reformers. Calvin, for example, thought that the James described by Paul as 'a pillar of the Church' (Gal. ii. 9) was in fact the son of Alphaeus; and, in the foreword to his commentary on the Epistle, he states that it is not for him to say whether this James or the ruler of the church of Jerusalem was its author. It would seem that Calvin hesitated about assigning the same degree of authority to an apostle other than Paul, if he was outside the number of the original twelve.

We can today attribute the Epistle with greater confidence perhaps than Calvin, to the ruler of the church of Jerusalem. Nothing that we are told in the New Testament about him militates against this ascription, and a good deal supports it. James heads the list of the four men who are described in the Gospels of Matthew and Mark as 'the brothers' of Jesus (Mt. xiii. 55). As Jesus was known as 'the carpenter' (Mk. vi. 3) and 'the carpenter's son' (Mt. xiii. 55), the probability is that He was the eldest of the family, and that He took over the business after Joseph's death. It is, moreover, unlikely, if He had been the youngest of the family, that, after the visit to Jerusalem when He was a boy of twelve was over, His parents should have gone a day's journey from the city before discovering that He was not in their company (Lk. ii. 44). As it was, the younger children were very naturally their primary concern, and His absence remained unnoticed. The view that Jesus was the oldest of the brothers is also supported by the *prima facie* meaning of 'first-born', *prōtotokos*, in Lk. ii. 7. It is unlikely that Luke would have used this word, if he had known that Mary had not given birth to other children, for the word *monogenes* (used in Lk. vii. 12, viii. 42 of 'only' children) lay ready to hand. We should also note that the natural implication of the words in Mt. i. 25 'knew her not till she had brought forth her firstborn son' is that, after that birth, normal marital relationships followed and other children were born. As A. H. McNeile remarks in his *Commentary on Matthew*, *ad loc.*, 'In the New Testament a negative followed by *heōs*, "until", always implies that the negatived action did, or will, take place after the point of time indicated by the particle' (see for example Mt. xvii. 9, xviii. 34; Mk. ix. 1). It is, we may again conclude, unlikely that these words, found in all Greek MSS. and omitted only in one old Latin MS. and the Sinaitic Syriac MS., would have been written by the Evangelist, if he had known that Mary was 'always-virgin', as later Christian writers dogmatically asserted. This view that the 'brothers' of Jesus were the younger children of Joseph and Mary, strongly advocated in the fourth century by Helvidius, was regarded as heretical chiefly because of the increasing value that came to be placed upon virginity, particularly by the writers of some of the apocryphal infancy gospels, and by Jerome. The latter assumed the virginity of Joseph as well as Mary. Dr. Vincent Taylor would seem to be wholly justified in asserting, in opposition to this, that 'the Helvidian view stands as the simplest and most natural explanation of the references to the brethren of Jesus in the Gospels'.[1]

After the rejection of the Helvidian view, the Western Church accepted uncritically Jerome's counter-view that the 'brothers' were cousins of Jesus;[2] while the Eastern Orthodox Church fell back upon a second-century view,[3] strongly supported by Epiphanius in the fourth century, that the 'brothers' were the children of Joseph by a former wife. This supposition has become popular among English scholars in recent years largely because of its advocacy by Lightfoot and Hort. It has,

[1] *The Gospel of Mark*, Macmillan & Co., 1952, p. 249.

[2] For full accounts and criticisms of the tortuous arguments which gave this view a semblance of truth see the Introductions to Mayor and Ropes.

[3] Origen mentions that the Book of James, an apocryphal Gospel, contained this view. The text of this *Book of James* or *Protoevangelium* can be read in *The Apocryphal New Testament*, M. R. James, O.U.P., 1924.

however, no direct New Testament support, and seems to have owed its origin, as did the view of Jerome, to an asceticism that was alien both to the spirit of Judaism and to the teaching of Jesus; and to that growing veneration for the virgin Mary which resulted in a spate of legends about her, and led to her worship as a 'mother-goddess'. Hence the insistence in some quarters that she was virgin not only *ante partum* but also *in partu* and *post partum*.

It is clear that the brothers of Jesus did not accept His authority during His earthly life. In Mk. iii. 21 we read that 'his friends' (the Greek expression *hoi par autou* would seem almost certainly to include members of His family) tried to restrain His activities 'for they said' (or perhaps 'people were saying') 'he is beside himself'. 'The family of Jesus', says Swete, in his *Commentary on Mark, ad loc.*, 'were doubtless inspired by a desire for His safety, but their interruption of His enthusiasm implied a want of faith in Him, cf. Jn. vii. 5.' Jesus certainly regarded it as an inevitable consequence of the fulfilment of His divine vocation that a new family should be created consisting of those who believed in Him; and to the creation of this wider family loyalty to His earthly family had to be subordinated (see Mt. xii. 48–50).

It was clearly a direct result of the resurrection of Jesus that the brothers, and James in particular, became Christians. Paul states in 1 Cor. xv. 5, 7 that the risen Christ 'was seen of Cephas, then of the twelve . . . after that, he was seen of James; then of all the apostles'. It would seem that, while Paul here differentiates between 'the twelve' and a larger number of 'apostles', he implies that James as well as 'the twelve' belong to the larger group described as 'all the apostles'; and the inference may reasonably be drawn that James became an apostle in virtue of his vision of the risen Lord (cf. Acts i. 22; 1 Cor. ix. 1). Whether the Jerusalem church accepted him as such immediately we do not know, but it is clear that very soon he became its recognized leader. For when Peter was miraculously released from prison, the first thing that he did on his return to the house of Mary, the mother of John Mark, was to tell his friends to go and give a report of all that he had told them 'to James, and to the brethren' (Acts xii. 17). And Paul notes significantly that, on his first visit to Jerusalem after his conversion, the special object of which was to make contact with Peter, he saw none of the other apostles 'save James the Lord's brother' (Gal. i. 19). This must have been a most memorable meeting for Paul, because then for the first time he would have been able to learn from one who was in a position to teach him, much that he must have surely wanted to know about Jesus of Nazareth.

James is represented throughout Acts as anxious that the Christian Church in its eagerness to evangelize should not sever too rapidly some of the practical links which bound it to its Jewish origins. He does not appear to have advocated that all Gentile converts should first be circumcised before becoming Christians, for the 'certain men which came down from Judaea and taught the brethren Except ye be circumcised after the manner of Moses, ye cannot be saved' (Acts xv. 1) may not have accurately represented James' position. But he does seem to have desired that Gentile Christians should not be encouraged to fraternize too freely at meals with Jewish Christians, and so offend the latter by not complying with Jewish food-regulations. In deference to his view on this subject Peter and Barnabas, much to the annoyance of Paul, abandoned their previous practice of 'eating with the Gentiles' at Antioch after 'certain had come down from James' (see Gal. ii. 12). It might perhaps be felt that James' somewhat exclusive attitude in this matter, at this early stage in the Church's development, is inconsistent with the strong condemnation of 'respect of persons', to be found in our Epistle. There, however, he is concerned specifically with the different kinds of welcome that might be given in the Christian assemblies to visitors of differing social or economic status. The question whether Jewish and Gentile Christians should meet together for communal meals is not under discussion; and, in all probability, that practice had become widely established by the time the Epistle was written. James presided over the conference held at Jerusalem to consider the terms of admission of Gentiles into the Christian Church and to arrive at a *modus vivendi* acceptable to both Jewish and Gentile Christians. The words in which he summed up the findings of the conference, 'My judgement is', give some indication of the authority he was recognized as possessing; and it was in his name and that of the other apostles that the letter containing the apostolic decree embodying the council's decisions was forwarded to the churches in Antioch, Syria, and Cilicia (see Acts xv. 19, 23).

It would seem that this acknowledged position of James as head of the Jerusalem church would give him the right to speak with authority to Christendom as a whole, as he does in his Epistle. It is worth noticing that the following linguistic resemblances have often been emphasized between James' speech at the Jerusalem conference and the circular letter containing its decisions on the one hand, and the Epistles of James on the other. The use of the word 'greeting', *chairein*, in Acts xv. 23 and Jas. i. 1 and nowhere else in the New Testament; the occurrence of the word 'visit', *episkeptomai*, in Acts xv. 14 and Jas. i. 27; the similarity of the expressions 'Men and brethren, hearken unto me' in Acts xv. 13 and 'Hearken, my beloved brethren' in Jas. ii. 5; and the parallel between the Septuagintal language 'upon whom my name is called' in Acts xv. 17 and 'that worthy name by the which ye are called' in Jas. ii. 7. Too much should not be made of these resemblances, however, for linguistic similarities can also be found between James' speech and other Epistles in the New Testament, where there is no question of similarity of authorship.

James is portrayed in Acts and the Pauline Epistles as anxious to effect a compromise in matters of secondary importance which would ease the tension, at a difficult period in the Church's history, between Jews and Gentiles. On the other hand, it is clear from his Epistle that, where there was any danger of compromise with the moral standards of paganism, he was unrelenting. The same desire for conciliation was shown by him on Paul's last visit to Jerusalem, when he prevailed upon the apostle of the Gentiles to show sympathy with four Jewish Christians who had taken a temporary vow, probably the Nazarite vow to abstain from wine and cutting the hair, by going with them into the Temple and by paying their expenses so that they could resume their normal way of life (see Acts xxi. 18–26). At this point the New Testament evidence for the life of James comes to an end.

Later traditions about James, which can only be briefly mentioned here,[1] contain much that is legendary, exaggerated and tendentious. When we leave the New Testament, we are very soon in the fanciful realm of hagiography. A passage in *The Antiquities* of the Jewish historian Josephus, published in 93, contains the sober statement that after the death of the procurator Festus in 61 and before the arrival of his successor Albinus, the high priest Ananus taking advantage of the interregnum arrested James on a charge of violating the law, and gave him up to be stoned.

Eusebius quotes a long passage from Hegesippus, who wrote *circa* 180, which contains the interesting information that James was known among the Jerusalem populace as 'the Just', or 'the Righteous One', because of his faithful observance of the Jewish law. It exaggerates, however, his ascetic tendencies, presenting him as a Nazarite from his mother's womb, who interceded in the Temple so frequently for God's people that his knees grew hard like a camel's; and it elaborates the story of his stoning, recording among a large number of more improbable details that, like Stephen, he prayed for his murderers at the moment of his execution. Hort agrees with Lightfoot 'in suspecting that this picture is drawn from an Ebionite[2] glorification of James'.

The apocryphal *Gospel of the Hebrews* exists only in such fragments of it as may be gleaned from Patristic writings. According to Jerome it contained a passage elaborating the story of the appearance of the risen Lord to James. In keeping with its marked *Jewish*-Christian bias it presents this as the *first* post-resurrection appearance, in opposition to the evidence of 1 Cor. xv. 7. It also asserts that James had vowed he would not eat bread from the hour that he drank the cup of the Lord

[1] The relevant passages are printed in full in the Introduction to Ropes.

[2] The Ebionites were an extreme early Jewish-Christian sect who rejected the Pauline Epistles and regarded James as their patron, falsely supposing that he was in opposition to Paul. Eusebius says that their name, meaning 'the poor ones', exhibits the poverty of their intellect.

till he saw Him rising from the dead; and that the Lord appeared to Him and said, 'My brother, eat thy bread, for the Son of Man has risen from them that sleep'. The story is obviously fictitious, assuming, as it apparently does, that James was present at the Last Supper.

What emerges clearly as history from this welter of later material is that James 'the Just' died a martyr's death at Jerusalem in the year 61.

The authorship of James the brother of the Lord is not only consonant with the note of authority which sounds throughout the Epistle, and with the possible echoes of the speech of James at the council of Jerusalem, but also with the extent to which the writer has obviously been profoundly impressed by the teaching of Jesus as we know it today in the Sermon on the Mount. The parallels between the ethical precepts of the Epistle and the dominical sayings, which are fully noted in the commentary, are not so close as to suggest direct quotation from any document. Rather does it seem as though James was giving fresh expression to truths He had often heard from the lips of Jesus Himself, before they became treasured documentary possessions of the Christian Church. If the brothers of Jesus were unable to accept the supernatural claims that He made for Himself during His earthly life, there is no reason to suppose that they were not deeply impressed by His moral earnestness and by the fresh and fuller emphasis that He gave to certain aspects of the moral law enshrined in Scripture. Nor need we doubt that they would have agreed with the verdict of his fellow-Galileans that 'he taught them as one that had authority, and not as the scribes' (Mk. i. 22). After the resurrection, James came to understand and to accept the doctrinal implications of the gospel about Jesus that was being proclaimed by the other apostles; but his own special contribution to the Church's message, and the single literary treasure that he was destined to bequeath to Christendom, were concerned with reinforcing some of the great moral truths on which his Brother had laid such stress. In other words, the ethical character of the Epistle and the comparative lack of strictly doctrinal teaching are not valid arguments against the traditional authorship.

A good deal has been made of the unlikelihood that a simple Galilean would have been able to write such good Greek as is found in this Epistle. There would, however, seem to be no real ground for supposing that an intelligent artisan living in Galilee in the first half of the first century could not have acquired skill in the use of the Greek language. 'The incongruity', writes an expert on the subject, 'of such a smart piece of Greek as the Epistle of James being written by a Palestinian Jew like James vanishes when we consider the bilingual character of the people of Palestine.'[1] Moreover, the excellence of the Greek should not be over-stressed; for, as the same writer says, 'The author of Hebrews, Luke and Paul, far surpass James in formal rhetoric'. The Epistle contains, it is true, some non-biblical expressions of a literary nature; nevertheless some of it can be readily translated into Hebrew,[2] though there are few actual Hebraisms, i.e. Hebrew idioms reproduced in Greek. With regard to the somewhat extensive vocabulary of a literary character found in the Epistle, it should not be forgotten that James resided at Jerusalem continuously, as far as we know, from the resurrection till his martyrdom some thirty years later, and that during this time his position as leader of the Christian Church in the city would bring him into contact with Jews and Christians from all parts of the world. We may also assume that he was not infrequently engaged in public speaking and debate, in which he could have developed the particular vernacular quality to be found in this Epistle. Its characteristic linguistic features are the frequent use of rhetorical questions; vivid similes and picturesque illustrations; imaginary dialogue; and constant appeals to the readers as a whole and to individual groups. The expressions 'my brethren', 'brethren', or 'my beloved brethren' occur fourteen times; and specific remarks are addressed to 'you adulterers', 'you sinners',

[1] *A Grammar of the Greek New Testament*, A. T. Robertson, p. 123. With this verdict J. H. Moulton agrees (*Cambridge Biblical Essays*, p. 487).

[2] See the Introduction to the Epistle of James by W. O. E. Oesterley in the *Expositors Greek Testament*, pp. 393–396.

'you double-minded', 'O vain man', 'thou that judgest thy neighbour', 'you rich', and 'you who say Today or tomorrow we will go into such a city'.

The author knew the Hebrew Bible in the Greek Septuagint translation; and he seems to have been familiar with some of the ideas contained in *The Wisdom of Jesus the Son of Sirach*. This book *Ecclesiasticus*, as it is usually called, was written about 180 B.C., and, after being translated, became part of the Greek Bible used especially by the Jews of the Dispersion. It was rejected from the Jewish Scriptures at the Council of Jamnia in A.D. 96, but continued to be regarded as inspired by Christians, though its authority was never wholly unchallenged. Jerome gave to this work and to the other books, which formed part of the Greek, but not of the Hebrew Old Testament, the title 'apocrypha'. They were books to be read privately for personal edification, and to be kept 'secret', i.e. not read in the public assemblies of the Church. Ecclesiasticus is found in the three oldest Christian Bibles that have come down to us, Codex Vaticanus, Codex Sinaiticus, and Codex Alexandrinus. Since the Reformation, Protestants have agreed that the Hebrew canon of the Old Testament alone has the authority of Scripture but they have varied in their judgment of the value of the apocrypha. For the most part their attitude has been that summed up in the sixth of the Thirty-nine Articles of Religion. 'The other books, as Jerome saith, the Church doth read for example of life and instruction of manners; but yet doth it not apply them to establish any doctrine.' One obvious reason for their rejection as canonical Scripture is the great stress laid in many of them upon the later Jewish doctrine of justification by works. Some of the possible parallels between the Epistle of James and Ecclesiasticus are noted in the commentary.

THE DATE OF THE EPISTLE

It is obvious that the problem of date is closely bound up with the problem of authorship. Those who regard the Epistle as pseudepigraphic, i.e. as published under a false name, very naturally assign it a late date, either the end of the first century or during the first half of the second; for, although Paul contemplated the possibility of letters being forged in his name (see 2 Thes. ii. 2), it is unlikely that pseudepigraphic literature would be circulated on any large scale during the life-time of the apostles.

If the traditional authorship is accepted, the Epistle could be dated at any time between 40 and 60. If it originated in the first half of the fifth decade, it would ante-date the Pauline letters and be the earliest document in the New Testament. Advocates of this early date, among whom Mayor has been the most influential, stress as determining considerations the absence of any reference to the admission of Gentiles into the Church, a subject with which James was much occupied later; the primitive character of the Church order and discipline presupposed, e.g. the use of the word 'synagogue' (ii. 2), and the lack of mention of any church officers except 'elders' (v. 14); and the generally Jewish character of the contents. None of these reasons are, however, conclusive. Arguments from silence must necessarily be very precarious when used in connection with a document as brief as this; and Jewish characteristics are not confined to the early books of the New Testament. No work is more thoroughly Jewish in character than the Revelation of John, but it is not usually dated earlier than the reign of Domitian (81–96).

Sanday's preference for a later date for the Epistle seems to show a sounder judgment. 'It implies', he wrote, 'too settled a condition of things. It is too little concerned with laying foundations. The distinctive doctrines of Christianity are presupposed. For this reason the Epistle should be put as late as it can be put in the life-time of James.'[1] It should be added that the apparent presence within the Christian communities addressed of more wealthy and perhaps intellectual members also does not favour an early date, as our evidence is that, in the first stages of the Gentile mission, 'not many wise men after the flesh, not many mighty, not many noble' were called (see 1 Cor. i. 26).

The question whether James, in the famous passage in the second chapter, is combating Paul's teaching in the Epistle to

[1] *Inspiration*, W. Sanday, p. 345.

the Romans, or *vice versa*, has been discussed at great lenght by scholars in connection with the date of the Epistle. If, however, it were to be supposed that either of the apostles was in opposition to the other on such a vital subject, there would be a dichotomy which would militate irremediably against the whole conception of a New Testament. The truth is that the two writers supplement one another. Nevertheless, it is more likely that James had in mind the perversions to which the Pauline doctrine of justification by faith early became subjected, when it was twisted in an antinomian direction, than that Paul should have directed his teaching in the Epistle to the Romans specifically against those who maliciously misinterpreted the Epistle of James by supposing that it advocated the Jewish doctrine of salvation by works. In other words, it is more probable that the Epistle of James is later than the Epistle to the Romans, which can confidently be dated early in the year 57. As Sanday went on to say after the passage already quoted: 'James is influenced by hearsay about Paul's teaching in Romans and false deductions from it. . . . If we suppose direct polemics between the two apostles, then both seem strangely to miss the mark. Each would be arguing against something which the other did not hold. It seems more true to the situation to regard James as, with a proper modesty, not imputing to his brother Apostle erroneous teaching, which he had not sufficient evidence to bring home to him, but taking a firm stand against abuses to which teaching such as that attributed to Paul seemed liable.'

The most probable date of the Epistle would seem to be *circa* A.D. 60. We may agree with Hort, 'No year can be fixed with any certainty: but 60 or a little after seems not far wrong. The essential point is not the year but the period, later than the more important part of Paul's ministry and writings.' In A.D. 60 Paul was a prisoner at Rome waiting his trial; the enthusiasm engendered by his Gentile missions was beginning to wane; heretical teaching of all kinds was beginning to raise its ugly head; and the world was beginning to recognize the Church as a potentially dangerous rival. Within eighteen months James was destined to be martyred. Within ten years, Jerusalem would be overthrown, the prestige of Judaism diminished, and the mantle of Jewish unpopularity fall upon the Christians. What was most to be feared at such a time was that, under the pressure of trials of every sort, Christians might fail to recognize or to give practical expression to the moral implications of their faith. Accordingly, James was inspired to exercise the authority that belonged to him as the leader of the mother church at Jerusalem by writing what is in every sense of the word a 'general' Epistle. Speaking sometimes with the fire and intransigence of an Amos; sometimes in the more reflective and aphoristic style of the Wisdom literature; sometimes in figurative speech such as may well reveal the lasting impression made upon him and, as we may also surmise from the Epistle that bears his name, upon his brother Jude, by the teaching of Jesus Himself; and always with vividness, energy, and dramatic power, he proclaims to the Christians of the second generation a message specially applicable to them but relevant to the Church in every age. For what he has to say is this. Religion divorced from morality, words without deeds, creeds that satisfy the head but never warm the heart, are vain. The wisdom that they exhibit is of the earth; the fire that kindles them is the fire of human pride.

SOME OTHER THEORIES OF THE ORIGIN OF THE EPISTLE

The view that the Epistle was originally a Jewish document, which has been given a Christian flavour by the insertion of the references to Jesus Christ in i. 1 and ii. 1, was put forward simultaneously and independently by L. Massebieau[1] in France in 1895 and F. Spitta[2] in Germany in 1896. Both critics were struck by the apparent total absence of anything specifically Christian in the Epistle apart from these two references, and by the fact that the sentences in i. 1 and ii. 1 would read equally well if the aforementioned references were omitted. This hypothesis, which at least has the merit of simplicity, has commended itself to very few scholars, chiefly on the ground that it is difficult to suppose that the imagined

[1] *L'épître de Jacques est-elle l'oeuvre d'un chrétien?*
[2] *Der Brief des Jacobus.*

Christian interpolator would have been capable of exercising such restraint! It has also been felt that the supposition that the Epistle is a hundred-per-cent Jewish in character is based too much on the argument from silence, viz., the lack of reference to Christian doctrines emphasized in other books, and is due to a failure to recognize the Christian assumptions that lie behind much of the Epistle and the implications of its teaching for Christian readers. 'There is no sentence in the Epistle', Ropes remarks, 'which a Jew could have written and a Christian could not.' The theory also assumes that the Epistle was not originally written in Greek. This is, however, very improbable, not least (to mention only a single point) because similar-sounding Greek words, bearing the same or a different meaning, are used as connecting links between consecutive sentences. Thus in i. 1–2 there is an association between 'greeting', *chairein*, and 'joy', *chara*.

With regard to the two verses, where the interpolator is supposed to have shown his hand, it is significant that in i. 1 Massebieau and Spitta do not agree about the extent of the interpolation. Spitta regards 'and the Lord Jesus Christ' as the inserted words, leaving an original 'James the servant of God'. Massebieau, on the other hand, confines the interpolation to 'Jesus Christ' leaving as the original the very awkward and most unusual expression 'James the servant of God and the Lord'. As for ii. 1, it is true that the words as they stand are not very easy to interpret (see the commentary, *ad loc.*); but it would seem that the addition of the words 'our' and 'Jesus Christ' by a Christian interpolator would in fact have been superfluous, and would only have succeeded in complicating a clause already quite capable of a Christian interpretation; for in 1 Cor. ii. 8 the expression 'the Lord of glory' by itself is used as a description of Christ.[1]

In 1930, the Spitta-Massebieau hypothesis was resuscitated by A. Meyer and Windisch.[2] As their work bears considerable resemblance to the typological explanation of Gospel origins

[1] For a full criticism of Spitta's view see Introduction to Mayor.

[2] A. Meyer, *Das Ratsel des Jacobus Briefes*. H. Windisch, *Die Katholischen Briefe*.

now much in favour in certain quarters,[1] some description of it here may not be out of place. In the Epistle of James, so these writers maintain, a Christian author has 'rehashed' an earlier Jewish document, in which the writer based a moral exhortation upon an allegorical exegesis of Gn. xlix. In that chapter, the patriarch Jacob before his death addresses a message to each of his sons, after whom the tribes of Israel were named. In this Epistle, another Jacob, Gk. *Iakōbos*, or James, addresses an exhortation to the spiritual descendants of Jacob, in which he emphasizes various moral truths suggested by the meaning of the names of members of Jacob's family, or by incidents in their lives. The following more plausible examples may serve to illustrate his method. *Joy* (i. 2) represents Isaac, whose name means 'laughter' (see Gn. xvii. 19). *Patient endurance* (i. 3, 4) is suggested by Rebecca, who was barren for twenty years after her marriage. 'The struggle for perfection' (i. 2–4, 12) is characteristic of Jacob, who wrestled with the angel (Gn. xxxii. 24–28). *Firstfruits* (i. 18) allegorizes Reuben, Jacob's 'first born'. The references to *hearing* (i. 19, 22) recall Simeon, whose name was derived from Hebrew *shāmā* to 'hear': while *anger* (i. 19, 20) and *over flowing of wickedness* (i. 21) are also illustrated by Simeon, whose massacre of the Shechemites, Jacob said, 'made his name stink among the inhabitants of the land' (see Gn. xxxiv. 30). *Religious* and *religion* (i. 26, 27) are equated with Levi, after whom the subordinate officers in the temple were named. *Judgment* (ii. 12) is the meaning of Dan (see Gn. xxx. 6). So the supposed solution to the problem goes on!

Some of the other suggested references are even more subtle and allusive, and can have been detected only after a much greater exercise of ingenuity! It is one of the surprising features of contemporary biblical criticism that such a method of exegesis should be regarded as a serious contribution to the problem of the origin of the Epistle of James, or of any other document in the New Testament. At least we might have expected that the author would have given his readers some

[1] e.g. *A Study of St. Mark*, A. M. Farrer, The Faith Press, 1951. *Studies in the Gospels*, edited by D. E. Nineham, Basil Blackwell, 1955.

clue as to what he was really doing;[1] and how strange it is that Christendom should have had to wait so long for the key to the understanding of his purpose!

A view of the origin of the Epistle which, like the two just mentioned, denies its integrity as the work of a single author but, unlike them, does not envisage an originally purely Jewish document, was suggested by F. C. Burkitt in 1924.[2] He assumes that the Epistle, as we now know it, is a free translation of a shorter Aramaic letter, which had been written by James, the brother of the Lord, to a small group of Christians probably resident in Jerusalem. The translator greatly expanded the original letter by adding the more peculiarly Greek elements in our Epistle, such as the expression 'the wheel of birth' (iii. 6) and the Septuagintal language of the Scripture references. James' letter, it is assumed, was not widely circulated at first, but was rescued from oblivion and saved for posterity by the action of the Greek-speaking Gentile Christians, who came to inhabit the newly built Jerusalem, named by the Romans Aelia after the emperor Aelius Hadrianus, who reigned from 117 to 138 and completed the destruction of the old city. These Christians came to look back with great veneration to the old church at Jerusalem, for they claimed to possess as a cherished relic the chair of its first 'bishop' James.[3] 'The Gentile church in the new pagan Jerusalem', says Burkitt, 'was rather like a new purchaser that has bought the Old Manor House, who after a while begins to collect old family portraits and souvenirs —coming at last to believe himself the genuine heir of the old line.' One of the souvenirs it managed to collect was the Epistle of James; but it was now turned by one of its members into a general Epistle 'to the Twelve Tribes in the Dispersion'. The chair of James has vanished, but the letter remains.

There would seem to be several difficulties about this

[1] The author of the Epistle to the Hebrews allegorizes the name Melchizedek; but the reader is made aware that this is what he is doing.

[2] *Christian Beginnings*, University of London Press, pp. 57–71.

[3] The tradition that James was ordained bishop of Jerusalem by Christ is first found in a second-century document, written to support the Ebionite heresy and known as *the Clementine Recognitions*. It is mentioned by Chrysostom in his comment on 1 Cor. xv. 7, and also by Eusebius.

imaginative reconstruction of the early history of our Epistle. In the first place, it would appear that Burkitt, with insufficient reason, has accepted as reliable the description of James found in the writings of Hegesippus.[1] It is obvious that the more James is believed to have conformed to the portrait there presented, 'the unshaven devotee who haunted the Temple colonnades', as Burkitt calls him, the less probable is it made to appear that he could have written an Epistle in such good, literary Greek as the letter which bears his name.

Secondly, Burkitt assumes that the Aramaic origin of portions of the Epistle can be detected from certain mistranslations. The only one he actually cites is iii. 6, where 'the world of iniquity' is supposed to be a mistranslation of an Aramaic word meaning 'the entrance of iniquity'. It is, however, not at all certain that this latter expression is any more intelligible than the much more forceful and original phrase found in all the MSS. of our Epistle (see commentary, *ad loc.*). And even if it be granted that the translator has in fact betrayed himself at this point, there are few other places, if any, where Burkitt's hypothesis forces itself upon the critic as the only possible solution. It is in fact denied by most scholars who, as we have had occasion to notice, regard the Epistle as it stands as the original work of a Greek-speaking Jewish Christian.

Thirdly, the passages cited by Burkitt as evidence for the existence of an earlier letter addressed by James to a particular congregation (ii. 2 ff., iv. 1, v. 4), do not of necessity demand this interpretation. The probability is that no section of the Epistle was written with one particular group of readers in mind. It is a general Epistle dealing with situations that might arise anywhere.

In a recent brief Introduction to the Epistle W. K. Lowther Clarke[2] dismisses the traditional authorship with the remark, 'Had the famous James been the author, the Church would presumably have felt no doubts regarding the book'; but he thinks it improbable that 'another man used his name, for he would surely have described the supposed author as "brother

[1] See previous reference to Hegesippus on p. 27.
[2] *Concise Bible Commentary*, S.P.C.K., 1952, pp. 914, 915.

of the Lord" or "apostle" '. He then draws attention without criticism to the suggestion that 'by James is meant the patriarch Jacob, who writes to his spiritual children. *The Testament of the Twelve Patriarchs*, a Jewish writing of the first century B.C. with Christian interpolations is an example of similar procedure.' The word 'similar' seems to imply that Dr. Lowther Clarke presupposes that this particular theory of the authorship necessitates the supposition that a Christian writer is adapting an earlier Jewish book. It is in fact another form of the Spitta hypothesis; for it would be very difficult to imagine a Christian writer himself using the name of the Jewish patriarch and describing him as 'a servant of God and the Lord Jesus Christ'. It is also very odd that Jacob should be presented as exhorting 'his spiritual children' to follow the examples of Jewish heroes such as Elijah and Job who were yet to be born. In *The Testaments of the Twelve Patriarchs* the sons of Jacob are content to refer to their own history and do not mention the outstanding figures of future generations.

Dr. Lowther Clarke favours, as a tentative conclusion, the authorship of an unknown James, 'a Greek-speaking Jew, who put his homilies into the popular letter-form, using much traditional Jewish material'; and he dates the Epistle 'any time between 70 and 100'. Though we reject this view, we nevertheless welcome Dr. Clarke's healthy reminder that arguments drawn from the silence of the Epistle about Jesus as Messiah, the cross and the resurrection are particularly dangerous. 'The author', he rightly says, 'was a Christian writing for Christians, and was at liberty to choose his own subject and treat it in his own way.'

COMMENTARY

CHAPTER I

a. The salutation (i. 1)

1. James, in sending greetings to his readers, is content to describe himself not by the title of any office he may be holding in the Christian Church, but very humbly by reference to his status as a Christian man. He is *a servant of God and of the Lord Jesus Christ.* His brother Jude similarly refers to himself as 'a servant of Jesus Christ', but notes in addition that he is a 'brother of James', thereby recognizing James as a more important person in the Christian community than himself (Jude 1).

James is not addressing a single group of Christians with whose circumstances he is especially familiar, but various congregations of Christians scattered far and wide throughout the Roman world. Together, these groups constitute the people of God who are continuous with the old Israel but consist of all, regardless of their nationality, who acknowledge Jesus as God's Messiah. The comprehensive term used to describe the old Israel in its totality, *the twelve tribes*, can, not unfittingly, be used as a symbolic description of the new Israel. Groups of the old Israel were to be found in the synagogues in many pagan cities as a result of the various transportations of Jews from the holy land by foreign powers; and such groups were known collectively as 'the dispersion' (see Jn. vii. 35; Acts ii. 5). In the same way groups of Christians had been *scattered abroad* as a result of the Christian missions which began with the banishment of numerous believers from Judaea after the persecution of Stephen (Acts xi. 19); and these could truly be described as 'of the Dispersion' (R.V.). To all of them James sends *greeting.*

The contents of the Epistle would seem to rule out the possibility that the description of the readers in this verse implies that they were unconverted Jews, or solely *Jewish* Christians. The symbolic description of them as the new Israel finds a parallel in 1 Pet. i. 1, where the addressees are called 'the exiles of the dispersion' (R.S.V.), and is in keeping with other New Testament descriptions of the Church.

b. Trials—the testing of character (i. 2–4)

2. Although the Christian *brethren* here addressed consisted of Gentiles as well as Jews, they all shared, as Christians, the hatred which was universally shown by pagans to the Jews; and from the beginning they were themselves subject to persecution, petty or otherwise, at the hands of their Jewish and pagan neighbours. This constituted a real challenge to the newly-converted Christian, the reality of whose faith is so often immediately tested by some form of external opposition. The Greek word translated *temptations*, *peirasmoi*, has the double sense of outward trials, and inward temptations. Outward trials very often become occasions of temptation to sin. In this verse the translation 'trials' (R.S.V.) is preferable; and the qualifying adjective *divers* (R.V. 'manifold', R.S.V. 'various') denotes that these trials may be of many kinds. But if the trials are manifold, so too is the grace of God with which the Christian can meet them (see 1 Pet. iv. 10). James therefore bids his readers every time they *fall into* (R.S.V. 'meet', the same word *peripiptō* being used as in the account of the man who 'fell among', i.e. 'encountered', robbers in Lk. x. 30) these trials to count it an occasion for unreserved rejoicing.

3. The reason for this call to rejoice is quite simply that, without trials, *faith* can never result in the tested character which should be the hall-mark of a Christian. The readers must fully understand that what is involved is *the trying* (R.S.V. 'testing') *of* their *faith*. Trials are the means by which their faith is proved; and such a testing *worketh* (i.e. 'works out', producing, as it were, a properly finished article) *patience*. This last word *hupomonē* has a more active content than the word 'patience'. Perhaps we may accept as the best rendering 'steadfastness' (R.S.V.).[1] A Christian must have staying power,

[1] See further the note on v. 11.

and this can be developed only in the face of opposition. Jesus said, 'In your patience ye shall win your souls' (Lk. xxi. 19, R.V.).

4. As the trials go on, so the 'steadfastness' must never flag. Steadfastness has, moreover, itself a task to accomplish, for it provides the atmosphere in which other virtues can grow. It must therefore be allowed to *have* its *perfect work* (R.S.V. 'its full effect'), that the Christian may be *perfect and entire*, pressing on to the complete and the fully-balanced life of holiness, *wanting nothing* (R.V. 'lacking in nothing'), never acquiescing in any shortcoming, in the effort to obey the Lord's command, 'Be ye therefore perfect, even as your Father which is in heaven is perfect' (Mt. v. 48).

c. Wisdom—God's answer to the prayer of faith (i. 5–8)

5. In this pilgrim's progress human cleverness and worldly wisdom are not only always inadequate but often definitely misleading. The Christian needs a different *wisdom*, a spiritual insight that will save him from slipping back into the follies of the unregenerate man. Those follies the book of Proverbs describes as the 'simplicity' of the 'fool', wise in his own eyes, who tries to live his life in his own way and resents correction by others. This higher wisdom is a supernatural gift; and all who are without it must ask God for it. That God will give it in response to prayer is a deduction from His nature, for one of His greatest characteristics is that He *giveth to all men liberally.* The last word, *haplōs*, combines the meaning of 'without guile' and 'without stint'. God is entirely free from any sordid or parsimonious calculations in His giving. He gives 'generously' (R.S.V.), a fine English word which refers, as does the Greek, both to the abundance of the gift and the gracious spirit in which it is given. God, moreover, *upbraideth not.* Sometimes, it is true, God does reproach mankind. Christ 'upbraided' his apostles for their disbelief on one occasion after His resurrection (Mk. xvi. 14). Here the expression has a special significance. 'It is added', Calvin finely comments, 'lest anyone should fear to come too often to God. Those who are the most liberal among men, when anyone asks often to be helped, mention their former acts of kindness, and then excuse themselves for the future. . . . There is nothing like this in God; He is ready to add new blessings to former ones without any end or limitation.'

6. Prayer for wisdom must be, like all prayer (see Mt. xxi. 21; Mk. xi. 24), the prayer of faith. He who prays for it must pray *nothing wavering* (R.S.V. 'with no doubting'). For if he doubts he sets up a disquiet in his soul which prevents him from leaning upon God—a disquiet comparable, in Hort's paraphrase of the simile used in this verse, to 'the restless swaying to and fro of the surface of the water blown upon by shifting breezes'. *Tossed* is too strong a translation, as the Gk. *ripizomenos* means literally 'fanned'.

7, 8. Not only does the doubting supplicant set up a restlessness within his soul, depriving himself of inward peace, but such a man (the expression *that man* has a somewhat contemptuous flavour) disqualifies himself from being the recipient of divine blessings; and he must not imagine that any other result is possible. The words *a double minded man unstable in all his ways* should probably be taken, as in R.V., in apposition to *that man*, and not as a separate statement as in A.V. The R.S.V. embodies them in the previous sentence and translates 'that person must not suppose that a double-minded man, unstable in all his ways, will receive anything from the Lord'; but this does not seem the most natural rendering in view of the order of the Greek words. Prayer involves the turning of the whole mind to God. We cannot be facing two ways at once when we are engaged in it. Hence the significance of the phrase *double minded.*

d. The Christian's status unaffected by poverty or wealth (i. 9–11)

9. This double-mindedness is essentially the mark of the man who is trying to serve both God and mammon. The Christian *brother*, therefore, is here bidden to find joy, not in the satisfaction of worldly ambitions, but in the new status into which he has been brought in Christ. Just as Paul bade the Christian slave rejoice in the fact that he was the Lord's freeman, and the Christian master remember that he was Christ's slave (see 1 Cor. vii. 22), so James, remembering that among the various groups of Christians to which he is writing there were great differences of economic status, bids *the brother of low degree*, who may not count for much in the earthly society to which he belongs, *rejoice in that he is exalted* in Christ to a very high level. Whatever may be his position in his earthly city, in the heavenly city into which he has now come as a Christian he is nothing less than 'a fellow-citizen with the saints' (see Eph. ii. 19).

10. Similarly, the rich brother is to rejoice that in Christ he has been brought down to a level where 'the deceitfulness of riches' (Mk. iv. 19) and the anxiety to amass and retain them are no longer primary or even relevant considerations; for in Christ he has learned to make a totally different evaluation of material prosperity. The new factor in his situation is that he has come to see that real wealth lies in the things that abide because they are eternal, and that it is the unseen things that have this characteristic (see 2 Cor. iv. 18). In comparison with these unshakable possessions material riches are recognized by him to be what in fact they are, transitory and uncertain. The one sure thing is that not only they but their possessor *shall pass away*, as surely as the flower of the spring grass suddenly drops after its brief existence.

11. The comparison of what is short-lived in human life with *the flower of the grass* is common in the Bible. Isaiah compared the frailty of 'all flesh' to the grass that withers and whose flower fades; and he contrasted it with the immutable and abiding word of God (see Is. xl. 7, 8). Peter quoted Isaiah's words to show that the new birth of the Christian is a birth to a life that is eternal, because the seed from which it springs is none other than the abiding word of God (see 1 Pet. i. 23–25). James, perhaps with the same passage from Isaiah in mind, here explains in effect why the *flower of the grass* is such an excellent simile for the transitoriness of human existence. In the holy land the grass is green only for a very short time. This is such a remarkable phenomenon that the mention by Mark that the five thousand were commanded to sit upon the *green* grass (Mk. vi. 39), and the record of John that 'there was *much* grass in the place' (Jn. vi. 10) are in fact specific indications of the time of year when the miracle of the feeding took place.

James draws attention to the almost instantaneous wilting of the grass when the sun is *risen with a burning heat*, and to the sudden transformation of a scene of beauty into one from which all the glory has departed. The word translated *burning heat*, *kausōn*, was also used for the south-east wind, the sirocco, which brought the heat and caused vegetation so often to perish. Jesus knew that this was a matter often discussed by His contemporaries. 'When ye see', He said, 'the south wind blow, ye say, There will be heat; and it cometh to pass' (Lk. xii. 55). The moral that James draws is that the rich man will die, like all other men, as surely as does the grass. The word *fade away* is particularly suitable in view of the simile. There is, moreover, great irony in the closing words *in his ways* (R.V. 'in his goings'; R.S.V. 'in the midst of his pursuits'). It is while he is engaged on one of his business journeys, mentioned again in iv. 13, that the rich man is struck down by what seems to be the ill-wind of fate.

e. Trial and temptation (i. 12–15)

12. It has already been stated that trials are the instruments, without which the Christian character cannot reach perfection, and that a divine wisdom is available for the believer in answer to prayer at every stage in the life of holiness. It is now asserted that *the man that endureth temptation* (R.S.V. rightly 'trial') is *blessed*, i.e. truly happy. The word *endureth* does not mean 'is forced to endure' but 'endures with that steadfastness to which reference has been made in verses two and three'. It is clear that outward trial and not inward temptation is at this point uppermost in the writer's mind, for, as Ropes truly says, 'Inner enticement to evil would have to be *resisted* not *endured*'.

True happiness is an eternal quality. While it can be enjoyed in part during this present life it always looks forward in hope to the fuller life beyond the grave which awaits the believer *when he is tried* (R.V. 'when he hath been approved'), and shown to be steadfast under affliction. This fuller life is here symbolically called *the crown of life*. The genitive is descriptive: *the crown* (literally 'garland' or 'wreath') consists of life; and the expression suggests 'the mark of honour to be given by the Great King to his friends' (Ropes). The *crown* here is not a sign of royalty, nor a prize as it is in 1 Cor. ix. 25, but a gift showing the approval of the divine Giver. 'It expresses', says Hort, 'in symbol what is expressed in words in the greeting "Well done, good and faithful servant" '. It was in this sense that Paul described his Thessalonian converts as his 'hope' and 'joy' and '*crown* of rejoicing' on the day of the coming of the Lord Jesus Christ (1 Thes. ii. 19). The love of the Christian for his Lord does not win for him eternal life as a reward to which he has a right, any more than does his faith. It is, however, an axiom of the Bible that God has abundant blessings in store for those who *love him*, keep His commandments, and serve Him faithfully whatever the cost may be (see Mt. xix. 28; 1 Cor. ii. 9).

13. Such steadfastness can never be shown, however, by those for whom the times of trial have become occasions for yielding to sinful temptation. There is always the danger in any temptation to evil, whether it arises from outward trial or not, that those who are so tempted will try to excuse themselves for yielding to it by blaming God on the ground that He is its author. The writer of Ecclesiasticus felt compelled, like James, to warn his readers against such blasphemy. 'Say not thou', he insists, 'It is through the Lord that I fell away. . . . It is he that caused me to err' (Ecclus. xv. 11, 12). The general teaching of the Bible as a whole on this subject would seem to be that, while God allows men to be tried, as Abraham's faith and Job's sincerity were tried, such trials may be used by the evil one, designated Satan or the devil, as temptations to do evil, though the devices of Satan can never thwart the ultimate purpose of God. Thus Jesus in the wilderness is tempted by the devil to pursue courses of action contrary to God's will, but in the end the devil retreats, having failed to deflect his would-be victim from His divine vocation (Mt. iv. 1–11). Similarly, Satan demands to have Peter that he may sift him like wheat; but 'his evil purpose stands in subordination to the divine purpose of perfecting apostleship' (Hort's comment on Lk. xxii. 31). What James is here denying is not that God tries men, but that He tries them *with evil intent* and so tempts them to sin. God by His very nature, he asserts, *cannot be tempted with evil*; He is incapable of any contact with evil at all. He cannot, therefore, be the cause of men's doing evil. *Neither tempteth he any man.* It is true that Scripture sometimes speaks of God's blinding men's hearts and giving them up to vile passions (see Rom. i. 24, 26). 'But', as Calvin so pertinently comments, 'Scripture does not assign to Him the beginning of this blindness, nor does it make Him the author of sin, so as to ascribe to Him the blame; and on these two things only does James dwell.'

14. Because James makes no mention in this passage of Satan as the tempter of mankind, it should not be supposed that he was unmindful of this view of the source of temptation or that he rejected it. It is his anxiety to deprive sinners of any excuse for their sin such as might lead them to throw the blame upon some external source, that causes him to stress exclusively the inward nature of temptation. The words *of his own lust* should probably be taken with both verbs as in R.S.V., which translates 'lured and enticed by his own desire'. Man is *drawn away* and *enticed* or 'ensnared' by his own sinful passions. The language is suggestive of a fish swimming in a straight course and then drawn off towards something that seems attractive, only to discover that the bait has a deadly hook in it. The Greek word translated *lust* (*epithumia*) has in the New Testament nearly always a bad sense, and the A.V. rendering is preferable to the more morally neutral 'desire' of the R.S.V. This verse, in fact, so far from being opposed to the doctrine of original sin, substantiates it. James would undoubtedly have agreed with the statement that 'the imagination of man's heart is evil from his youth' (Gn. viii. 21). Lustful desires, as our

Lord so clearly taught (Mt. v. 28), are themselves sinful even when they have not yet issued in lustful actions.

15. It is of the breaking out of these lustful desires into concrete sins that James seems to be thinking when he says that *lust* after it *hath conceived*, i.e. after it has received the assent of the will, *bringeth forth sin.* He is using at this point the language of child birth. Just as a child is alive before the actual moment of its birth, so sin does not begin to be sinful only when it is manifest in a specific, visible action, though some such sinful action is bound sooner or later to emerge, once the lustful thought has been entertained and cherished. *Sin,* James adds in conclusion, thinking not of one isolated sin but of the accumulation of sins that constitutes the sinful life, *when it is finished* (R.V. 'fullgrown'), *bringeth forth death,* which is the exact antithesis of the blessed state alluded to in verse 12 as the *crown of life.*

f. God the author and giver of all good things (i. 16–18)

16. So far from God's tempting men with evil intention, He is the source of all good; and, because this is such an important truth about God, James earnestly and tenderly appeals to his *beloved brethren* not to err in this matter. The form of expression here used 'introduces a pointed utterance' (Ropes). Paul uses it, for example, as a preface to the dictum 'God is not mocked' (Gal. vi. 7).

17. In this verse two different Greek words are translated by *gift.* The former *dosis* usually denotes the act of giving, as in Phil. iv. 15; and the latter *dōrēma* the thing given. It is probable that the words are not mere synonyms repeated for rhetorical emphasis, for no instance has been found in the papyri of the purely concrete use of the former.[1] Assuming therefore the predicative force of *good*, the meaning may be that 'all giving is good', even, we may suppose, the gifts which evil men give their children (see Mt. vii. 11); and yet in comparison with God's gifts all other gifts lack perfection, and are always to some extent marred by impurity of motive. It is

[1] See Moulton and Milligan, *Vocabulary of the New Testament*, s.v.

only *from above*, i.e. from heaven (see iii. 15; Jn. iii. 31), that *every perfect gift* comes.

The reason why gifts *from above* are *perfect* is that they descend from the *Father of lights*. God is the Creator of those heavenly bodies which give light to the universe and are vital to the maintenance of physical light. But unlike them there is with God *no variableness or shadow of turning*. The Greek word *eni* translated *is* implies that there is no possibility of any such change. The sun gives its light to the earth in varying measure 'now the full light of noon, now the dimness of twilight, and at night no light at all' (Ropes); but there is no variation with God (see Mal. iii. 6). The light of His truth and the light of His holiness remain constant (see 1 Jn. i. 5); He always wills what is best for His children, and He always bestows such gifts as they need for His purpose to be fulfilled.

There is considerable variation in the MSS. in the last words of the verse, though all printed editions of the Greek Testament read *ē tropēs aposklasma* translated *neither shadow of turning* (R.V. 'neither shadow that is cast by turning'; R.S.V. 'or shadow due to change'). If this usual reading is adopted, the A.V. translation might be read as implying that there is not the smallest trace of variation in the Godhead, which makes good sense but gives too slight a meaning to the Greek word *aposkiasma*. The R.V. and R.S.V. renderings suggest with more probability that it is the shadow on the earth caused by the apparent revolution of the sun that the writer has in mind. The R.S.V. marginal version 'variation due to a shadow of turning' reflects another reading *hē tropēs aposkiasmatos* found in the fourth-century Codex Vaticanus, the first hand of the fourth-century Codex Sinaiticus, and a fourth-century papyrus fragment found at Oxyrhynchus in 1914. In this variant it would seem that the definite article should be substituted for the conjunction *or* (Greek *hē* for *ē*),[1] and that together with the following nouns, both in the genitive case, it defines more clearly in a single phrase what is envisaged in the variation just mentioned. Such variation consists in, or may be observed in the shadow which is cast on the earth and is short or long as

[1] The absence of breathings in ancient Greek MSS. permits this.

the sun appears high or low in the heaven. (For a full discussion of the readings see Ropes, *ad loc.*)

18. Of all God's gifts that of new birth to His children is the greatest and most important. This spiritual begetting is *of his own will.* No other consideration influences Him in this matter except His purpose to choose from the rest of His creatures a people who will be 'holy and without blemish before him', adopted as His sons through Jesus Christ (see Eph. i. 4–5). Men are made His sons when they hear and respond to the gospel of salvation, here called *the word of truth* as in Eph. i. 13; Col. i. 5. The Christians living in James' day are described as *a kind of firstfruits* of this new creation, probably because there would be a greater harvest to come as a result of subsequent Christian missions. It is unlikely that the expression *firstfruits* refers to Jewish as distinct from Gentile Christians, for the Epistle would appear to be addressed to all Christians alike (see comment on i. 1). The significance of the metaphor lies in the fact that the first fruits were offered to God and were therefore sacred (see Lv. xxiii. 10). The old Israel was 'the firstfruits of his increase' (Je. ii. 3); consequently such language could very naturally be used with reference to the members of the Christian Church.

It should be noted that Hort interprets *us* in this verse of mankind in general, and considers that the reference is to the supremacy given by God to man over other creatures. On this view *the word of truth* is an allusion to the word of God spoken to man at the creation (Gn. i. 28). But, as Ropes remarks, 'the objection which seems decisive against it is that the figure of begetting was not used for the creation, whereas it came early into use with reference to the Christians who deemed themselves "sons of God" '.

g. Hearers of the word (i. 19–21)

19. For '*wherefore . . . let every man be*' the most ancient MSS. have 'Ye know this', or Know this[1] . . . but let every man be', as in R.V. and R.S.V. This gives a more forceful meaning: 'You

[1] For the grammatical point here, whether *iste* is indicative or imperative, see *Grammar of New Testament Greek*, J. H. Moulton, Vol. II, p. 222.

are aware of (or 'rest assured of') the heavenly origin of your new birth, but you must see to it that it reflects itself in your personal conduct.' Because God is the originator of the new birth, the characteristics of the new life which that birth inaugurates must be obedience to God, and a readiness to listen to His word as it is found in the records of His revealed will in Scripture and in what He may speak to His children through the voice of conscience. Christians must be *swift to hear*. Conversely they must be *slow to speak*, not rushing hastily to proclaim God's word to others before they have really paid attention to it themselves. They must also be *slow to wrath*, for an essential condition of listening to God is that the mind should not be distracted by thoughts of resentment, ill-temper, hatred, or vengeance, all of which are comprised in the general term *the wrath of man*.[1]

20. There would seem to be two thoughts underlying what is said in this verse about man's wrath. First, men who are wrathful do not practise that kind of conduct which alone is right in God's sight. On the contrary, by allowing free play to passion they render dispassionate, and therefore just, decisions in human affairs impossible. What God requires is that man should 'do justly' (Mi. vi. 8); and man's wrath, fitful and wayward as it is, prevents the fulfilment of this requirement. Secondly, *the wrath of man* prevents God's righteous actions from being vindicated by the Christian; for it becomes more difficult for others to lay hold of the truth that the Judge of all the earth is essentially moral and Himself does what is right (see Gn. xviii. 25), if His servants fail to show righteousness in their conduct.

21. *Wherefore*, i.e. because docility and a receptive spirit are to be distinguishing characteristics of Christians, James bids them first *lay apart* (taking it off from themselves as though it were a dirty garment) all that is filthy in God's sight. Man's attempts to live his life in his own way, to make and follow his own moral standards, or to vindicate himself before God by his own efforts are all alike doomed to failure, for 'all our

[1] See further the author's *The Biblical Doctrine of the Wrath of God*, p. 9.

righteousnesses are as filthy rags' (Is. lxiv. 6). The man who has been restored as a Christian to a state of rightness with God must have these 'filthy garments' taken from him and be clothed with a change of raiment signifying his new status (see Zc. iii. 4). Together with the *filthiness* there must also be laid aside any 'hang-over' of previous pagan habits. It is true that the Greek word here used, *perisseia,* usually means 'surplus'; and to that extent the translation *superfluity of naughtiness* might seem to be accurate. The writer cannot, however, mean that it is only the surplus of naughtiness or wickedness that must be laid aside. It is, therefore, probable that the word here has the same sense as *perisseuma,* 'remainder'. Every converted Christian brings with him into his new life much that is inconsistent with it. This has to be laid aside, that he may give himself more completely to the positive work of receiving *with meekness the engrafted* (R.V. rightly 'implanted') *word.* He has already, it is assumed, received assurance of salvation through faith in Jesus Christ; but the ethical implications of the gospel he has accepted, and the growth in holiness which it involves are matters to which he must give humble and constant attention; for, as Calvin truly said, 'doctrine must be transfused into the breast and pass into conduct, and so transform us as not to prove unfruitful'.

The *word* of God is here designated 'implanted' because, when it falls in the human heart upon soil that has been prepared by the Holy Spirit to receive it, it is welcomed and takes root and so transforms the soil that out of it those beautiful Christian virtues can spring which are the reflections of the character of Jesus Himself. Paul calls them 'the fruit of the Spirit' (Gal. v. 22). As a result of this the full and final salvation of the Christian is certain. The word rooted in his heart *is able to save* his *soul.*

h. Doers of the word (i. 22–25)

22. But if a Christian must listen to God's word before he attempts to proclaim it, he must not be content with a listening that is merely passive. Christianity is essentially a life to be lived. Hence the injunction in verse 22 *Be ye* (the Greek *ginesthe* has the implication 'Make sure that you are') *doers . . . and not hearers only*. The word translated *hearers*, *akroatai*, was used especially of those who were regular in listening to lectures, but who never became real disciples. So it is possible to hear God's word constantly proclaimed in lessons from Scripture and in sermons, and to regard such hearing as an end in itself, so that the message heard never becomes translated into deeds accomplished. This, says James, is a form of self-deception. We are indeed to be hearers, for nothing takes the place of the regular listening to God's word; but we are not to be *hearers only*. Jesus pronounced a benediction not upon those who hear the word of God, but upon those who 'hear the word of God, and keep it' (Lk. xi. 28).

23, 24. Words that are merely heard and never allowed to take root in the heart are soon forgotten, however valuable in themselves they may be; and the benefit gained from such hearing is both imperfect and short-lived. Hence the suitability of the simile here used of looking into a *glass* (R.V. rightly 'mirror', for ancient looking-glasses were made of metal). The face that a man sees as he looks into a mirror is his own face; but it is never quite the same from day to day. For, though it is always his *natural face*, the face with which he was born (Vulgate, *vultum nativitatis suae*), it is constantly being changed as it reflects the experiences of his life. He tends, moreover, to look at it often but never for very long. *He beholdeth himself, and goeth his way*, or as Mayor well renders, bringing out the change in the Greek tenses, 'Just a glance and off he goes'. And, if he does see glimpses on his countenance of the ravages being wrought by sin, sickness, anxiety, or the inevitable passage of time, his instinct is to banish such a vision quickly from his memory. He turns at once to other things: *straightway he forgetteth what manner of man he was.*

Hort translates 'the face of his creation', and assumes the meaning to be that the man has a temporary glimpse of his face as it would have been if sin had not come in to 'deface' it. But, though this gives a sense suitable to the context, for the man who is a hearer only of the Word does receive a fleeting vision of what God meant him to be, and of what by God's grace he is capable of becoming, it would seem more natural to suppose that the contrast here is, in Mayor's words, 'between the face which belongs to this transitory life and the reflection as seen in the Word of the character which is being here moulded for eternity'.

25. The true listener is one who takes the trouble to *look into* what he hears and to consider its implications for practical living. The Greek word here used, *parakuptō*, seems in the New Testament to have the sense of 'peering into' because there is something important which the viewer desires to see, even though it may be difficult for him to see it and grasp its meaning all at once. Thus Peter and Mary 'peer into' the empty tomb on Easter morning (Jn. xx. 5, 11). Similarly, Peter says that angels desire to 'peer into' the contents of the apostolic gospel (1 Pet. i. 12).

What the true believer sees as he peers is *the perfect law of liberty.* It is a *perfect* law because it is the law of the new covenant which Jeremiah prophesied would be written by God in men's inward parts and upon their hearts (see Je. xxxi. 33). It is not therefore something imposed upon the believer from without in the form of a code of external rules and regulations. It is not for him a dead letter but a living power. It would seem to be called the *law of liberty* partly because it enables men to find their true freedom in the service of God's will, and partly because the believer accepts it without any compulsion. The Christian loves God's commandments and is eager to obey them. After hearing them, he does not go away at once, anxious to forget them as soon as possible. On the contrary, he *continueth therein.* He remains with them (Gk. *parameinas*), and makes them his daily study and delight. As a result he becomes a *doer of the work* (R.S.V. 'a doer that acts'), and cannot fail to find happiness in what he does. 'He shall be blessed in his doing.' 'If ye know these things,' Jesus said to His disciples after commanding them to follow His example and wash one another's feet, 'happy are ye if ye do them' (Jn. xiii. 17).

i. Religious observance (i. 26, 27)

26. The 'doing' in which the Christian will be *blessed* can, however, be spoilt, as has already been suggested in verse 19, by a failure to *bridle the tongue.* It is very easy, James here reminds his readers, for a man to *seem to be religious* (R.V. rightly 'thinketh himself to be', for the Gk. *dokei* means 'seem in his own estimation'), simply because he is often engaged in religious observances and in the performance of religious duties. These may be perfectly good in themselves, but their value may be lost because the 'religious' man fails to control his speech in the ordinary relationships of life. When this happens, such a man *deceiveth his own heart.*

The word translated *religious*, *thrēskos*, and the cognate noun translated *religion*, *thrēskeia*, seem to describe a scrupulous attention to the details of formal worship. Such a person may be very careful to use the right words when he is performing a religious ceremony, but very careless in his speech at other times. No particular examples are here given of such unbridled speech, but the reference is perhaps mainly, if not exclusively, to slander: for, as Calvin pertinently comments, 'he who seems brilliant with some outward show of sanctity will set himself off by defaming others, and this under the pretence of zeal but really through the lust of slander'. Such *religion*, says James, is *vain*, Gk. *mataios*, because it fails to please God, which should be the primary object of religion. He may have had our Lord's words in mind: 'This people draweth nigh unto me with their mouth, and honoureth me with their lips; but their heart is far from me' (Mt. xv. 8; cf. Is. xxix. 13).

27. The man who is scrupulously 'religious' may take care to see that everything connected with the ritual of his worship is *pure* and *undefiled*; but, as God so often stated through the mouth of His prophets, the externals of religion, however punctiliously performed, are quite unacceptable to Him unless accompanied by a genuine desire on the part of the worshipper to render sympathetic and practical service to his fellow-men. James is not in this verse giving a complete definition of religion, any more than the prophet in Micah vi. 8 is giving a full account of what God requires of man. 'James', comment,

Ropes, 'had no idea of reducing religion to a negative purity of conduct supplemented by alms giving.' Similarly Moffatt remarks,[1] 'Even the practical James, who encountered spurious forms of religious love, never dreams of opposing them by anything like an ethic which should be a substitute for religion'. James is, in effect, restating the truth which our Lord emphasized when He said that, on the day of judgment, He would recognize as His followers those who had rendered service to Him by visiting the sick among His brethren, and would fail to recognize those who had withheld that service (Mt. xxv. 36, 43). James uses precisely the same word here for *visit*, *episkeptomai*, when he says that *pure religion and undefiled* in the eyes of the Father-God is to *visit* those who are bereft of human fathers.

God Himself is revealed in the Bible as 'a father of the fatherless, and a judge of the widows' (Ps. lxviii. 5); and He expects those whom He adopts as His sons to be, in the words of the writer of Ecclesiasticus, 'a father unto the fatherless, and instead of a husband unto their mother' (Ecclus. iv. 10). It is perhaps not without significance that, when Jesus restored her son to the bereaved widow of Nain, the people were led to say 'God hath *visited* his people' (Lk. vii. 16); and it is certainly pertinent to remember that one of Jesus' strongest condemnations of certain of the Pharisees was that they enriched themselves by embezzling the property of widows (see Mk. xii. 40).

But along with this personal service, so strongly stressed as an essential function of true religion, there must also be a perpetual striving after personal holiness. The believer must never be blind to his duty to express his faith in love, but at the same time, in the midst of all the distracting and demoralizing influences of the world around him, which lies wholly in the evil one (see 1 Jn. v. 19, R.V.), he must keep himself pure by continual remembrance of the demands of the all-holy God. The lambs that were offered under the Old Testament sacrificial system had to be without blemish: so the Christian must *keep himself unspotted from the world* that he may offer himself a holy and living sacrifice acceptable to God. 'Keep thyself pure' was one of Paul's last admonitions to his young friend Timothy (1 Tim. v. 22).

[1] *Love in the New Testament*, Hodder & Stoughton, 1929, p. 127.

CHAPTER II

a. Respect of persons (ii. 1–7)

1. A further example is here given of the futility of any profession of Christianity which does not express itself in right conduct. To claim to be worshipping Him who came on earth to reveal to mankind the love of God by laying down His life for all sorts and conditions of men, and at the same time to separate from the family for whom Christ died a particular section as objects of favouritism because of their more fortunate economic status—this is a perversion of true religion. Such behaviour is entirely inconsistent in one who holds *the faith of our Lord Jesus Christ*, i.e. who professes to believe in Jesus Christ as his Lord. The expression *the Lord of glory* is found in 1 Cor. ii. 8 and elsewhere in the New Testament, and presumably means 'the Lord who now reigns in glory'. There is, however, in the Greek text no repetition of *the Lord* as in A.V., R.V., and R.S.V.; and it is difficult to see why the writer, if he had intended to connect *of glory* with *the Lord*, should not have placed the words in juxta-position. As it is, *the glory* is found in the genitive case immediately after 'our Lord Jesus Christ'.

It may well be then that *the glory* should be taken in apposition to *Jesus Christ*. He is *the glory* in the sense that He fully reflected on earth, within the necessary limitations of His incarnate life, the nature of God Himself. He was Immanuel—God with us. As the glory of Christ was revealed in conditions of poverty and humiliation, such a reference would be especially suitable to this particular context where respect for the rich at the expense of the poor is so strongly deprecated. In this interpretation, first suggested by Bengel and subsequently adopted by Mayor and Hort, *the glory* is almost a descriptive title for Christ; and although such a title is not found elsewhere, what is implied in it is a truth unfolded in several passages (see especially Lk. ii. 32; Jn. i. 14, xvii. 5; Heb. i. 3).

Some commentators, including Calvin, have regarded *the glory* as a genitive of origin, and, giving it the sense of 'esteem' which the Greek word *doxa* often has, have connected it with *respect of persons.* In this interpretation, it is respect of persons arising from falsely esteeming certain human beings as greater than Christ Himself, against which James is warning his readers. The order of the words in Greek does not, however, naturally suggest this connection.

Others have taken *the glory* as a genitive of quality, and connected it with the words *our Lord Jesus Christ* in the sense of 'our glorious Lord Jesus Christ'; but this seems an unduly fulsome expression. Even Ropes, who advocates it, remarks, 'it is not an altogether happy expansion of "the Lord of glory" in 1 Cor. ii. 8'.

Respect of persons is specifically forbidden in the Mosaic law, particularly in judical decisions (see Dt. i. 17).

2, 3. James now gives a specific illustration of the kind of way in which this *respect of persons* might express itself. Two non-Christian visitors might enter the Christian *assembly* (R.V., more literally, 'synagogue', the word denoting either the place of assembly or the company assembled). One might be wearing *a gold ring* (R.S.V., perhaps better, 'with gold rings') and *goodly apparel* (R.V. 'fine clothing'; perhaps, in modern English, 'smartly dressed'); the other might be a beggar *in vile raiment* (R.S.V. 'in shabby clothing'). Both ought to be welcomed, for both might perhaps be won for Christ; but they should be welcomed as equals in the assembly where all are equal in the sight of God. There would, however, be a temptation for those who have not fully thrown off the false values of their pre-converted life to *have respect to* (R.S.V., 'pay attention to', the Greek *epiblepō* meaning to 'look with favour upon') the former of the two visitors by conducting him to a specially good and comfortable seat. *In a good place* translates the Greek adverb *kalōs*, which could also have the force of our idiomatic 'please'; hence the R.S.V. 'Have a seat here, please'.

The text of the words imagined as being spoken to the

poorer visitor is uncertain. The oldest reading, that of Codex Vaticanus and the Latin Corbey MS. which may reflect a fourth-century text, is probably 'Stand or sit here . . .',—a rough invitation to the man either to stand anywhere or, if he prefers a seat, to sit on the floor close to the speaker's foot-stool! *Stand thou there* (just where you are), *or sit here* and R.V. 'Stand thou there, or sit' would seem to be later variations of the original text.

4. There are two things fundamentally wrong with this behaviour. First, it shows a divided allegiance, a hypocritical desire to serve God and mammon, a 'double-mindedness' such as was condemned in i. 7, 8. The translations *Are ye not then partial in yourselves* and R.S.V. 'have you not made distinctions among yourselves' take the verb *diekrithēte*, which is passive in form, as though it had an active sense. R.V. 'are ye not divided . . . ?' should probably therefore be accepted. Codex Vaticanus omits the word *not*; in which case, the sentence instead of being a question is an effective affirmation, 'Ye are divided.'

Secondly, those who differentiate between rich and poor in this way show themselves to be judges with vitiated motives. *Judges of evil thoughts* is misleading, for it might imply that they were judging the evil thoughts of others. The genitive is a genitive of quality. They are themselves 'judges with evil thoughts' (R.V.).

5, 6. But, further, this *respect of persons* is unrealistic. It fails to take account of the facts of the situation. In the first place, *the poor of this world* (R.V., following the MSS. which read *the world* in the dative case instead of the genitive, translates 'poor as to the world', i.e. poor in the judgment of the world, or in regard to what the world considers wealth) have been chosen by God *rich in faith* (R.V. 'to be rich in faith'). They are 'rich towards God' (see Lk. xii. 21); rich in the gifts of the Spirit; rich with the only wealth that God reckons as true wealth. It is not that God has limited His choice to the poor, but that, as a matter of history, they have been His first choice (see Lk. i.

52; 1 Cor. i. 26). He has both exalted them in the present circumstances of their life and given them hope for the future; for He has made them *heirs of the kingdom which he hath promised to them that love him.* Such right of inheritance has not been promised as a reward for their love. The truth is that God has called them in order that they may love Him; and the inheritance is in heaven ready for those who love Him. These poor are in fact 'the poor in spirit', to whom Jesus said the kingdom of heaven belongs (see Mt. v. 3; Lk. vi. 20); for it is God's good pleasure to give them the kingdom (see Lk. xii. 32).

How disgraceful, then, to depress still further those whom God, by the exercise of His sovereign power of choice, has been pleased to exalt! There is great indignation in the words *But ye have despised* (R.V., better, 'dishonoured') *the poor.*

Secondly, it would show a very strange sense of the fitness of things to single out for special flattery those among whom the most violent oppressors of the Christians were to be found, It is odd, as Calvin comments, to honour one's executioners and in the meantime to injure one's friends! So James reminds his readers of what was actually happening in the world. *Do not rich men* (R.S.V. 'Is it not the rich who') *oppress you?* In v. 4, 6 James gives an example of the kind of oppression he has in mind. That the rich often found it in their interests to oppress the Christians in the early days of the Church can be seen from Acts iv. 1–3, where the rich Sadducees are said to have 'laid hands on' Peter and John; from Acts xiii. 50, where at Pisidian Antioch the 'chief men of the city' were stirred up to persecute Paul and Barnabas; and from Acts xvi. 19, where at Philippi the hitherto wealthy owners of the girl with the spirit of divination dragged Paul and Silas into court. Moreover, the direct cause of the uproar at Ephesus was the unpalatable truth that the spread of Christianity was leading in certain industries to a decline of profits (see Acts xix. 23–41).

7. But the supreme offence of these wealthy oppressors, which makes them such strange objects for flattery, is that they *blaspheme that worthy name by the which ye are called* (R.V. margin, more close to the Greek, 'which was called upon you', perhaps at baptism). *That worthy* (R.V. 'honourable') *name* is the name of Christ. It was apparently an ancient Hebrew custom for the names of ancestors to be 'called over' a man's offspring. Thus Jacob, resting his hands upon Ephraim and Manasseh the two sons of Joseph, said 'let my name be named on them, and the name of my fathers Abraham and Isaac' (Gn. xlviii. 16). Similarly, Christ's name is named at baptism over all who belong to Him. It is an 'honourable' name, because it brings honour to all who are called by it.

b. The royal law (ii. 8–13)

8. The A.V., in the opening phrase *If ye fulfil*, does not translate the Greek particle *mentoi*. R.V. gives it its usual adversative sense and translates 'Howbeit if you fulfil'. It is generally supposed by commentators who take the particle in this sense that James has in mind an imaginary excuse which the flatterers of the rich might bring forward. By honouring their rich visitor they might claim to be obeying the commandment to love their neighbour as themselves. But, as Hort remarks, 'it is hardly credible that so absurd a plea, of which there is not the least hint in the text, should be contemplated by James; and it is difficult to find any other way of satisfactorily justifying an adversative sense'. Hort therefore suggests that *mentoi* should be regarded as a stronger form of Gk. *men* and taken as giving emphasis to the following verb. R.S.V. follows Hort in this, and translates 'If you really fulfil', the implication being that they are not fulfilling it if they show partiality.

God has 'revealed' very clearly in *the scripture* (viz. Lv. xix. 18) *the royal law* which His servants must follow. The *neighbour* to be loved as oneself tended to be limited in practice to fellow-Jews. Our Lord, on the other hand, insisted that all who need our help in any way are to be regarded as 'neighbours' (see Lk. x. 29–37). This law is called *royal*, partly because it is the law of the kingdom of God, given by the supreme King Himself, and partly because, in its very comprehensiveness, it is the law that governs all other laws concerning human relationships. *Ye do well* might almost appear an understatement, when we remember that the observance of this *royal law* is stated by our Lord to be an essential part of the condition of eternal life (see Lk. x. 27, 28).

9. *Respect of persons* is wholly incompatible with this *royal law*, for it is expressly forbidden in one of the subsidiary laws by which the 'royal law' was applied in the Mosaic legislation to the various contingencies of life (see Lv. xix. 15). Every time respect of persons is shown, a sin is perpetrated, sin being essentially violation of the divine law (see 1 Jn. iii. 4). Moreover, the law itself shows up the perpetrators as *transgressors*. For the archaic *and are convinced of the law* read R.V. 'being convicted by the law'. The teaching of this verse has obviously a special relevance for the Christian today as he tries to show the reality of his religion in the often difficult but pressing problems of social, industrial and racial relations.

10. The great truth contained in this verse is that men must not 'pick and choose' when they are confronted with the moral law of God. They must not try to excuse their failure to observe one part of it by pointing to their observance of other parts. God, says Calvin, will not be honoured by exceptions. He will not let us subtract from the laws we do not like. We may not separate what He has joined together. Some parts may seem to us to be less important than others, but they are all parts of the divine law which must be accepted *in toto*. Men can, therefore, never claim to be righteous because they keep a part of God's laws. *For whosoever shall . . . offend* (R.V. 'stumble') *in one point, he is guilty of all*. And it is just man's utter failure to obey that law in its entirety that makes it necessary for his salvation to depend, not on his own righteousness, but upon the righteousness of Another—Jesus Christ.

11. All the commandments contained in the second half of the decalogue are concerned with *the royal law* quoted in verst 8. Failure to observe any one of the commandments is therefore failure to observe the law as a whole. James quotes two of these commandments in the order found in the Septuagin- version of Ex. xx. 13 as found in Codex Vaticanus. The come mand *Do not commit adultery* is also placed before *Do not kill* in some MSS. at Mk. x. 19. There is no need therefore to find some subtle reason for this unusual order by supposing, as Hort does, that James acknowledges that those who dishonoured the poor might in fact be observing the law to the extent that they refrained from adultery, but that they were failing to see that they were violating the law against murder as that law was interpreted by Jesus. It would seem that James is giving a purely hypothetical case and quoting the commandments with no special consideration for their order. *If thou commit no adultery, yet if thou kill, thou art become a transgressor of the law*; for the law is fundamentally a unity being an expression of the undivided will of a single Lawgiver.

12. Christian love is shown in both speech and action. James accordingly urges his readers to show obedience to *the royal law* both in what they say and in what they do. In giving preferential treatment to the rich, and thereby passing judgment upon the relative importance of different classes of society, they are only too likely to forget the judgment that awaits themselves. They must *so speak* and *so do, as they that shall be judged.* Moreover the nature of the law by which they shall be judged ought to cause them to be especially merciful toward others. This law, as has already been stated in i. 25, is *the law of liberty.* It has been freely accepted by all who have submitted to the yoke of Christ, for they know that God in His mercy has through Christ delivered them from the penalties attached to their past disobedience; and they also know that, by their union with Christ, a new liberating power is now at work within them making it possible for them to render obedience.

13. The Christian need not therefore have any fearful expectation of judgment. He must, however, constantly remember the conditions laid down by Jesus Himself as essential if the prospect of that judgment is to be faced with equanimity. The *merciful*, said Jesus, shall obtain mercy (Mt. v. 7); those who refrain from judging will not themselves be judged adversely (see Mt. vii. 1). On the other hand, those who are not prepared to forgive the trespasses of others will find that their own trespasses will be unforgiven (see Mt. vi. 15); and the debtor, rid in God's mercy of his own immense load of debt, cannot expect such mercy to be extended to him for ever if he is unwilling to cancel an infinitely smaller debt of one of his fellows (see Mt. xviii. 23–25).

This teaching of Jesus is echoed in the two affirmations of this verse. First, the truth is stated negatively. *He shall have judgment without mercy* (R.V., more literally, 'judgement is without mercy to him'), *that hath shewed no mercy.* Then follows the positive assertion. *And mercy rejoiceth against* (R.V. 'glorieth against'; R.S.V. 'triumphs over') *judgment.* Mercy shown on earth by the justified sinner, who has himself been the object of God's mercy, is a sure ground for confidence that for him the sting of the final judgment will be found to have been already drawn (see Mt. xxv. 34–40). If *and* is omitted, as in R.V., following the most ancient MSS., the statement becomes an axiom capable of wider application.

c. Faith and works (ii. 14–26)

14. As mercy has been shown to be an inevitable product of love, so, James now proceeds to demonstrate, where loving action is conspicuous by its absence, there is irrefutable evidence that real faith is lacking. To make this vital point perfectly clear, in case anyone should ever try and divorce faith and love, James asks two rhetorical questions, the implied answer to both of which is 'Most certainly not'. It is important to note that he does not say 'though a man has faith' but *though a man say he hath faith, and have not works.* Such a professed faith, being totally lacking in results, is useless; and James shatters the confidence of those who think it possesses any value, just as surely as Jesus did when He said, 'Not every one that saith unto me, Lord, Lord, shall enter into the kingdom of heaven; but he that doeth the will of my Father which is in heaven' (Mt. vii. 21; cf. xxv. 45). This 'wordy' faith is not worth calling faith at all; for real faith unites a man with Christ so that his thoughts and actions come under the control of His Spirit. Spurious faith has no saving power. The translation *can faith save him?* is misleading, and fails to bring out the force of the Greek definite article. We should read either R.V. 'can that faith save him?', or R.S.V. 'Can his faith save him?'

15, 16. James here gives a very forceful, if hypothetical, illustration of the negative character of the faith which is a mere confession of the lips and never results in effective action. He imagines Christians in dire need of the necessities of life being sent away by fellow-Christians, not after being given *those things which are needful to the body*, but with a curt command to do something totally impossible. Such persons might be male or female, here called *brother or sister*, for all who are disciples of Jesus are bound by close family ties. They might also *be* (the Greek word *huparchōsin* suggesting, perhaps, that this is the state they are in when they first become members of the Christian community) *naked* (R.S.V., rightly, 'ill-clad', as in Mt. xxv. 36 and Jn. xxi. 7) and *destitute of daily food.* In such a case as this *what doth it profit?*, James asks indignantly, if *one of you say unto them, Depart in peace* (i.e. 'Good-bye'), *be ye warmed and filled* (i.e. 'Get some clothing and nourishing food').

In the expression *notwithstanding ye give* there is a transition from the singular 'one of you' to the plural *ye*, for James assumes that all members of the brotherhood would be responsible for these callous remarks even though only one of them might give utterance to them.

17. Such words are dead words because, so far from applying a practical remedy in a desperate situation, their only effect would be to depress still further those who were already chilled and starving. In the same way, James concludes *faith . . . is dead, being alone*; i.e. faith, which has not in itself, as an integral element in its composition, the power and the desire to meet the infinite pathos of human life with something of the infinite pity which God has shown to man in Jesus Christ, is not faith at all.

18. The difficulties of this verse, which has always been a *crux interpretum*, are largely due to the lack of punctuation in ancient MSS. and the absence of such aids as are afforded to modern readers by marks of quotation. The problems may be summarized as follows:

(i) Who is the person speaking in the expression *a man may say*? Is he speaking as a friend or as an opponent of James? And could it be James himself?

(ii) How much is to be included in what this *man* is imagined as saying? Only the words *Thou hast faith*? Or the clause *Thou hast faith, and I have works*? Or the rest of the verse as well?

(iii) To whom do the personal pronouns refer in the clause *Thou hast faith, and I have works*?

If we are to suppose that a friend is speaking as a kind of representative of James, then the whole of the remainder of the sentence should probably be taken as a quotation addressed to the man attacked in the previous verses who made a profession of faith without works; and the sense would be such as is presupposed in the following paraphrastic translation of R. A. Knox. 'We shall be inclined to say to him, Thou hast faith, but I have deeds to show. Show me this faith of thine without any deeds to prove it, and I am prepared, by my deeds, to prove my own faith.' This interpretation is very similar to that given by Mayor and others. It is open, however, to the serious objection that the expression *Yea, a man may say*, like Paul's 'But someone will say', is most naturally understood as introducing the remarks of an objector. Moreover, it might appear to attribute to James the acknowledgment that this man really has faith, when the aim of the previous verses has been to show that his faith is no faith at all.

We should assume, then, that it is an objector who is speaking, and that what he is supposed to be saying is *Thou hast faith, and I have works*: these words alone should be put in quotation marks in a modern translation, as in fact they are in R.S.V. But it would seem that by *thou* the objector does not mean 'thou, James', and that by *I* he does not mean 'I, the objector'; for, if this were so, it would have surely been more natural for the sentence to have read 'Thou hast works and I have faith', an inversion of the nouns which is found in the old Latin Corbey MS. but nowhere else. More probably, as Ropes remarks, 'the pronouns do not refer to James and the objector, but are the equivalent of "one", "another", and are merely a more picturesque mode of indicating two imaginary persons'. The objector is saying in effect, that some people do in fact claim to have the gift of faith and others the ability to do good works; and he might even be insinuating that they could appeal to such a passage as 1 Cor. xii. 10 in support for such 'diversity of gifts'. In this case, the words *shew me thy faith without* (R.V. 'apart from') *thy works, and I will shew thee my faith by my works* are James' rejoinder to the objector. He condemns strongly any dichotomy of this kind between faith and works, and challenges him to produce, if he can, an example of real faith which finds no expression in works; and he adds, without any thought of self-justification, that he himself will have no difficulty in showing the reality of his own faith by his actions.

19. James addresses once more the mere professor of faith, and admits, for the sake of argument, that he might give intellectual assent to the doctrine that there is one God and one only, *Thou believest that there is one God.* Or, it may be, that the reference is to the doctrine of the unity of the Godhead, as in R.V. and R.S.V. 'that God is one'. Whichever translation we adopt this is a doctrine of primary importance, and to acknowledge its truth is admirable; hence James adds *thou doest well.* But, in itself, it has no saving power whatever. 'Knowledge of God', comments Calvin, 'can no more connect a man with God than the sight of the sun can carry him to heaven.' It is faith, not knowledge, which enables man to draw near to God, and so to achieve the primary aim of religion; and because man is a sinner, his approach must be through a Mediator; faith in that Mediator is therefore an essential element in his faith in God.

The devils also (R.S.V. 'even the demons') acknowledge the existence and the transcendence of God; but the only effect it has upon them is that they *tremble* (R.V. 'shudder', i.e. in terror). Particularly did the demons shudder when faced with Jesus. They knew that they were doomed to perish ultimately at the hands of the omnipotent God, and were conscious that in Jesus they were confronted, prematurely so it seemed (see Mt. viii. 29), with their destroyer. 'What have we to do with thee, thou Jesus of Nazareth?' they cried, 'art thou come to destroy us?' (Mk. i. 24). Those who have true faith, James here implies, though they rightly feel a sense of awe when they draw nigh to God, do not shudder in fear before Him. They approach with boldness to the throne of grace (see Heb. iv. 16). God, moreover, expects them to give evidence of their faith, not by shaking in terror but by acts of charity.

20. The expression *wilt thou know* introduces a fresh stage in the argument. James is about to bring forward Scripture proof for the thesis that *faith without works is dead* (R.V. and R.S.V. 'barren', following a different, and probably the original reading, as there would have been a tendency for scribes to alter 'barren' to 'dead' in view of verse 26). 'Barren' (Gk. *argos*) means 'ineffective', and hence, in this context, 'unproductive of salvation' (see verse 14); the same word is used in Mt. xii. 36 where Jesus states that every 'idle' word will have to be accounted for on the day of judgment. The *vain man* (R.S.V. 'foolish fellow') addressed is anyone who is so devoid of spiritual understanding that he does not see that faith which never results in works is merely a sham.

21. The wholly false deduction sometimes drawn from this verse, that there is a radical contradiction between what James is saying and what Paul says in the Epistles to the Galatians and Romans, is due to the failure to see that James is not using the word *justified* with reference to that occasion alluded to by Paul (Rom. iv. 3; Gal. iii. 6) when Abraham is said to have 'believed in the Lord; and he counted it to him for righteousness' (Gn. xv. 6, R.V.). That initial justification of Abraham was at a time when neither Ishmael nor Isaac were born, and when, humanly speaking, there seemed no possible likelihood that God's promise to Abraham that his seed would be as the stars of heaven could ever be fulfilled. Nevertheless, Abraham believed that God meant what He said. James is here speaking not of this original imputation of righteousness to Abraham in virtue of his faith, but of the infallible proof, given in the incident recorded in Gn. xxii, that the faith which resulted in that imputation was real faith. It expressed itself in such total obedience to God that thirty years later Abraham was ready, in submission to the divine will, to offer *Isaac his son.* There is emphasis as well as poignancy in these three words, because without Isaac it was evident that God's previous promises to Abraham could not be kept. James is not therefore defining the mode of justification as Paul is so careful to do. His aim is to destroy the pretence of those who imagined they had faith, when there was no evidence in the way they behaved to show that their faith was alive. *Justified* in this verse means in effect 'shown to be justified'.

The translation *when he had offered* is apt to be misleading, because it might be read as a confirmation of the erroneous view that the offering of Isaac was the cause for the imputation of righteousness to Abraham by God. The Greek aorist participle is better rendered as in R.V. 'in that he offered'.

It is interesting to notice that James, addressing a Christian audience made up of both Jews and Gentiles, can speak of Abraham as *our father.* Although Gentiles were not physically descended from Abraham, nevertheless as Christians, who were justified by faith in the crucified Son of God, they are Abraham's seed, for they have a faith similar in character to that of Abraham (see Gal. iii. 16).

The Epistle to the Hebrews also draws attention to the faith shown by Abraham in his willingness to offer Isaac (see Heb. xi. 17); but it is there mentioned as an outstanding example in the long line of heroes, who under great trials never lost their belief in the reality of the unseen or their conviction that God would implement His promises. The question of the method by which righteousness was imputed to Abraham is not discussed in Hebrews any more than it is in James.

22. The translation *Seest thou* (R.V. 'Thou seest') *how faith wrought with his works* is difficult. The Greek verb here used, *sunergeō*, means 'work with', and so the literal meaning is 'faith co-operated with his works'. We are not, however, to suppose that it was Abraham's faith plus his works which now brought about his justification for the first time, but rather that faith co-operated with him and enabled him to perform acts of obedience, here called *his works*. The fact that the verb is in the imperfect tense suggests that this co-operation was always going on. Faith never exists in total isolation. It is a living thing which produces living things in the form of actions performed in obedience to the will of the living God.

When James says *and by works was faith made perfect*, he does not imply that Abraham had previously had a weak or loveless faith, and that now, by this act of obedience, it had become strong. There are in reality no degrees of justifying faith. Men either believe or they do not; and there is no faith which does not issue at once in loving obedience. Faith is, however, called upon from time to time to show its integrity in special acts of obedience; and this happened when Abraham was called to offer Isaac his son.

23. The words here quoted from Gn. xv. 6, *Abraham believed God, and it was imputed unto him for righteousness*, though they referred specifically to something that happened thirty years before the incident narrated in Gn. xxii, are nevertheless regarded as being *fulfilled* in Abraham's readiness to sacrifice Isaac, for there is a sense in which they were prophetic of that event. There had to be, in the providential ordering of things, occasions when the truth that Abraham's faith had been counted unto him for righteousness became transparently clear; and this was one of them, though by no means the only one.

James also draws upon further Scripture proof in his desire to underline the reality of the righteousness imputed to Abraham. *He was called the Friend of God*. In 2 Ch. xx. 7 Abraham is called God's 'friend for ever'; and in Is. xli. 8 God calls Israel 'the seed of Abraham my friend'. The meaning of the expression '*friend of God*' seems to be that God did not hide from Abraham what He proposed to do (see Gn. xviii. 17). Abraham was privileged to see something of the great plan which God was working out in history. He rejoiced to see the day of the Messiah (see Jn. viii. 56). Similarly, because Jesus unfolded to His apostles, particularly in the discourses in the Upper Room at Jerusalem, the divine secrets entrusted to Him, He was able to call them His friends. 'Henceforth', He said, 'I call you not servants; for the servant knoweth not what his lord doeth: but I have called you friends; for all things that I have heard of my Father I have made known unto you' (Jn. xv. 15).

The meaning is certainly not that Abraham 'earned the title of God's friend' because of his readiness to sacrifice Isaac, as R. A. Knox's translation states; any more than we should infer that the apostles of Jesus earned by their obedience the right to be initiated into the secrets of the divine will, and so be styled Jesus' 'friends'. Both in the case of Abraham and of the apostles it was entirely due to divine grace that they were able to receive a title of such honour and dignity.

24. James now addresses all his readers, and invites them to draw for themselves the obvious inference from the story of Abraham, particularly from the part of it relating to the sacrifice of Isaac. The inevitable conclusion is that, while it is faith that justifies, for James never denies this fundamental truth, faith is never static. Faith is a practical response to the divine initiative. It is an answer to a heavenly call, and the call is always a call to obedience. Therefore obedience, expressing itself in action, is the inevitable and immediate issue of faith. *Ye see then how that by works a man is justified, and not by faith only.* In other words, the life of sanctification dates from the moment a man is justified by faith, when he surrenders himself to Jesus Christ as His personal Saviour, through whose saving death apart from any merit of his own he is counted righteous in the sight of God; but the life of sanctification is not a life of faith only; it is a life of what might be called faith-obedience.

25. This section of the Epistle might presumably have ended with the conclusion reached in verse 24. James is led, however, to give an additional proof of the truth he has been propounding. In order to show that it is universally applicable and allows of no exceptions, he cites the case of one who was a Gentile, a woman, and a prostitute. He seems conscious that in Rahab he is taking an example from the bottom end, as it were, of the social ladder; for the words *also was not Rahab the harlot* should probably be translated 'Was not even the harlot Rahab?'

The Epistle to the Hebrews also draws attention to Rahab's action in welcoming, concealing, and expediting the departure of the spies sent by Joshua to Jericho, but as an expression of her faith, as a result of which she 'perished not with them that were disobedient, having received the spies with peace' (Heb. xi. 31, R.V.). James does not mention her faith; but he assumes that his readers know the story of how she acknowledged the supremacy of the God of Israel. 'The Lord your God', she said to the messengers, 'is God in heaven above, and in earth beneath' (Jos. ii. 11). But this was no 'barren' faith such as that condemned throughout this second chapter of James, for it created an immediate desire to further the purposes of the God of Israel by prompt and effective action. She *received the messengers* in a friendly manner, and *sent them out*, enabling them to escape with impunity. It could therefore be as truly said of her, as it was said above of Abraham, and in the same sense as it was said of Abraham, that she was *justified by works*. Instead of *when she had received . . . and had sent them* we should read the R.V. 'in that she received . . . and sent them', the Greek aorist participle having the same force as in verse 21.

26. It has been implied throughout this section that the mere profession of faith is in itself a dead thing, for, if it is unproductive of good works, it is not really faith at all. Not unnaturally therefore, in this final verse, James bluntly asserts that such faith is comparable only to a corpse, from which the breath of life has vanished. He could scarcely have expressed the truth by a stronger or more conclusive image.

CHAPTER III

a. The responsibility of the teacher (iii. 1–5a)

1. Not unnaturally James follows the statement that *faith without works is dead* by the reminder that *works* are not to be limited to actions. Words are also works. Indeed, much of the work of the world is accomplished through the medium of words. This is particularly true of the work of teachers (A.V. *masters*). Hence James sounds the warning 'Let not many of you become teachers' (R.S.V.). Often the words of teachers leave an indelible impression for good or evil upon receptive and immature minds. For them the warning of Jesus is especially relevant: 'By thy words thou shalt be justified, and by thy words thou shalt be condemned' (Mt. xii. 37). The ambition of many Jewish parents to have their sons trained as Rabbis, and the desire of many young men to enjoy the privileges and exercise the power that the office of Rabbi brought with it, led our Lord to give this *caveat* to His disciples 'Be not ye called Rabbi: for one is your Master, even Christ; and all ye are brethren' (Mt. xxiii. 8). James may well be echoing this injunction, with special reference perhaps to those known as 'teachers' in the Early Church, references to whom are made in Acts xiii. 1; 1 Cor. xii. 28; and Eph. iv. 11. James seems to regard himself as such a 'teacher', for he uses the first person plural when he states the main reason why there ought not to be large numbers of Christians eager to take up this work. '*We*', he reminds those already engaged in this occupation, '*shall receive the greater condemnation*' (R.V. 'judgement').

Teachers are continually engaged in passing judgments, both moral and intellectual. The very nature of their work makes them critical, sometimes severely critical. James warns them that all who have professed to point out to others the way in which they should live, will receive greater condemnation than the rest of men if they have failed to walk in that way themselves. This verse is not, however, meant to discourage those who believe themselves to be called to take up this vital work. On the contrary, by pointing out the special dangers and responsibilities of this great vocation it is in fact enhancing its dignity. While it would seem unnatural to see here, with Calvin, a warning *solely* against moral censoriousness, nevertheless all should learn from it to abstain from passing judgment upon their fellows; for, as Calvin well reminds us, 'it is an innate disease of mankind to seek reputation by blaming others'.

2. Self-examination, James implies, instead of stopping short at the sins of speech, should begin with them; and when it does begin with them it becomes at once apparent that we all offend. The translation *offend* seems to have come straight from the Vulgate; the Greek word *ptaiō* is intransitive and means 'stumble' (R.V.), i.e. 'sin'. It is surely significant that when Paul is giving Scripture proof for the assertion that 'all are under sin', he makes the following composite quotation from the Psalms: 'Their throat is an open sepulchre; with their tongues they have used deceit; the poison of asps is under their lips: whose mouth is full of cursing and bitterness' (Rom. iii. 13, 14). James here states this truth the other way round *If any man offend not in word, the same is a perfect man.* A close parallel is 'Blessed is the man that hath not slipped with his mouth, and is not pricked with the multitude of sins' (Ecclus. xiv. 1). The *perfect*, or innocent, man is the man who has his tongue completely under control; for, as the tongue is the hardest of all the members of the human body to control, it follows that in controlling the tongue he possesses the power *to bridle the whole body*, which sin uses as the medium of its self-expression.

The implication of this verse is not that men should plunge themselves into prolonged and unnatural periods of silence in an endeavour to reach perfection, but rather that they should learn under the Holy Spirit's guidance 'to bring into captivity every thought to the obedience of Christ' (2 Cor. x. 5); 'for out of the abundance of the heart (which includes the mind) the mouth speaketh' (Mt. xii. 34), and 'from within' proceed not only evil actions but evil words (see Mk. vii. 21–23).

3. The expression *Behold*, so characteristic of Semitic writers, is used six times in this Epistle, and always to introduce a vivid illustration. Although there is a variant reading in the MSS. here, followed by R.V. and translated 'Now if', the A.V. reading, in view of the author's usage, should probably be retained. What is true of horses, he asserts, is also true of men. If we control their mouths we can obtain their obedience, and *turn about their whole body*, guiding them in the direction we desire. The word translated *bits* (*chalinous*) is the noun from the verb *bridle* (*chalinagōgeō*) used in the previous verse; it denotes 'the reins', or 'the whole bridle', as well as the actual 'bit'. R.V. translates, somewhat unnaturally, 'If we put the horses' bridles into their mouths'. R.S.V. returns to the A.V. rendering.

4. A further illustration, often coupled with the former by ancient Greek authors, of the dominion exercised by the tongue over a man's whole life is taken from the rudder of a ship. Just as the rider's pressure on the bit changes the direction of his horse, so pressure upon *a very small helm* (R.V. 'rudder') alters the course of the largest ships. As it is not clear why the size of the ships and the fact that they are *driven of fierce winds* should be so closely connected, it may be, as Hort suggested, that we should translate *and* as 'even' with the sense 'even when they are being driven by strong winds'. In other words, the rudder has some effect even in a gale. *Whithersoever the governor listeth* is a threefold English archaism, rightly changed by R.S.V. into 'wherever the will of the pilot directs'.

5a. The little bit and the little rudder achieve big results. So does the little member of the human body, the tongue. It *boasteth great things*. There is a sense in which the tongue can be said to possess great things of which it can *legitimately* boast. History affords numerous illustrations of the power of great oratory to encourage the depressed, to rouse the careless, to stir men and women to noble action, and to give expression to the deeper human emotions. The magic of words has played an incalculable part in the long story of human endeavour and human suffering. It may be, therefore, as many modern commentators have suggested, that at this point James is not meaning to disparage the tongue but to draw attention to the magnitude of its achievements, and that the translation should be 'has great things to boast of' (R.S.V. 'boasts of great things'). But the Greek word here used, particularly if read as a compound verb *megalauchei* as in most MSS., and not as two separate words, the adjective *megala* and the verb *auchei*, usually denotes arrogant boasting, 'talking big'; and it is probable that it is 'the tongue that speaketh proud things' (Ps. xii. 3) that James is here describing.

b. The havoc wrought by the tongue (iii. 5b–12)

5b. The word *Behold*, introducing a fresh illustration, suggests that the second part of this verse should really be the beginning of a new verse, if not of a new paragraph. James wishes to illustrate the destructive power of the tongue in individual lives and in human relationships by the truth that it needs only a tiny spark to set on fire a great mass of material. Accordingly he first draws attention to this phenomenon. The word *hulē* translated *a matter* (A.V. margin and R.V. 'wood'; R.S.V. 'forest') is used either of living or dead wood; and the picture here suggested may be either that of a woodland blaze or of a fire in a timber-yard.

6. In this very difficult verse, after explicitly identifying the tongue with *a fire*, James describes its devastating effects. The punctuation adopted by A.V. makes an awkward sentence and necessitates the insertion of the word *so* not in the original. It is better therefore with R.V. and R.S.V. to put a full stop after *fire*, and to take the words *a world of iniquity* as the predicate of the verb in the following clause. 'The tongue is a world of iniquity in our members.' The expression *world of iniquity* is difficult. If it is construed as in A.V. the meaning would seem to be 'the sum total of iniquity' (as in the Vulgate translation *universitas iniquitatis*). Apart, however, from the hyperbolical nature of such a statement, it is very doubtful if the Greek word *kosmos*, translated *world*, can bear this meaning. If, on the other hand, the R.V. punctuation is followed, then the interpretation would seem to be 'The tongue represents the unrighteous world in our members'. In other words, all the evil characteristics of a fallen world, its covetousness, its idolatry, its blasphemy, its lust, its rapacious greed, find expression through the tongue. In consequence, the tongue *defileth the whole body*, it pollutes the entire personality.

But there is more to it than this. This pollution is no temporary phenomenon; it is not something that can be easily erased; for the tongue exercises its evil influence continuously through the whole course of human life. It *setteth on fire the course* (A.V. margin and R.V. 'wheel') *of nature*. The wheel, because its function is to revolve and because it is a circle always revolving on the same axis, was a common symbol among the ancients both for the changeableness and the completed 'round' of human life (for examples see Ropes and Mayor, *ad loc.*). Each human life rolls onward, as it were, from birth to death through many phases and changes, in order to complete its allotted 'cycle. It would appear to have been in some such sense that the early Latin translators, probably rightly, understood these words. Hence their translation *rotam nativitatis nostrae*. The evil influence of the tongue spreads out from the axle to the entire circumference of the 'wheel' at every moment in its revolving course. This interpretation takes the word *nature*, Gk. *genesis*, in its primary sense of 'birth', and relates the expression to the life of the individual from birth onwards. The early Syriac translators extended the meaning to encompass all generations of men, and paraphrased 'the successions of our generations which are like wheels'. Other commentators take *nature* in its secondary sense of 'creation', but it is difficult to see in what sense the tongue can be said to set on fire created things.

Finally, the fire with which the tongue is here equated, is said to be itself *set on fire of hell*. There are two kinds of fire. The fire which purifies and illuminates is kindled by the Holy

Spirit and descends from above (see Acts ii. 2, 3). The fire which inflames human passion and infects human life throughout its entire existence is kindled by the devil and comes from beneath. It is, in fact, the fire of Gehenna, in which the unrepentant sinner is ultimately punished (see Mt. v. 22, xviii. 9).

7. At the original creation man was given 'dominion over the fish of the sea, and over the fowl of the air, and over every living thing that moveth upon the earth' (Gn. i. 28; cf. Gn. ix. 2). It is implied in this verse that this dominion has been retained. All types of creatures, though not all of any one type, can, it would seem, be tamed, and many have actually been tamed by men. The most savage of wild beasts, the fishes which inhabit a different element, the birds which are so quick in their flight, and the serpents with their death-bringing poison have all alike succumbed to human skill. Yet because of the fall man has lost dominion over himself. He is no longer master in his own house. In particular, the tongue, given him by God to enable him to communicate with and to enjoy fellowship with other men and to give articulate praise to his Maker, has become the means by which he so often deceives his fellows and dishonours his Maker. The first words recorded in the Bible as spoken by fallen man after his expulsion from Paradise are in the nature of a lie (see Gn. iv. 9).

8. Humanly speaking complete control of the tongue is an utter impossibility. It is evil in itself and intractable. The A.V. *an unruly evil* follows the reading *akatascheton* of the later Greek MSS. It is somewhat weak, as it adds nothing to what has already been said. The R.V. translates the stronger reading *akatastaton* of the older MSS., 'a restless evil'. This suggests a reason why the tongue, unlike the beasts, birds, serpents, and fishes, cannot be tamed. It is never sufficiently at rest for it to be brought fully under control. It is, moreover, as James adds, echoing the words of Ps. cxl. 3, *full of deadly poison.*

9. The fact that sometimes the tongue is used for a beneficial and worthy purpose such as giving glory to God, so far from exonerating it from general condemnation, only draws attention to its inherent inconsistency. The highest use of human speech is the praise of Him who is acknowledged to be 'the Lord and Father' (so R.V., translating the oldest MSS.) of mankind. The later reading, followed by A.V., *God, even the Father*, may be due to the influence of Mal. ii. 10. 'Have we not all one father? hath not one God created us?' But when the same tongue proceeds to *curse men which are made after the similitude of God*, it is in effect cursing God Himself and obliterating the previous act of blessing. In fallen man the image of God has become marred because of sin; and this is perhaps why James says here 'made after the likeness of God' (R.V.), rather than made 'in the image of God' (Gn. i. 27). It is important to remember that, in spite of all the sin and evil inherent in human nature, the likeness of God is still reflected to some extent in every child of the human race. The word translated *are made*, *gegonotas*, is in the perfect tense, which means that men still have upon them the marks of their divine origin. 'He then', comments Calvin, 'who truly worships and honours God, will be afraid to speak slanderously of men.'

10. Not only is the inconsistency of the same tongue blessing God and cursing men something contrary to His revealed will. It is also, James here asserts, *contra naturam*. The word translated *ought* (*chrē*) implies that, quite apart from any divine revelation about the difference between right and wrong, such incongruity is out of keeping with the fitness of things.

11. Any traveller, James implies, should be able to recognize that by no conceivable possibility can *a fountain send forth* (R.S.V. 'pour forth') *at the same place* (R.V., rightly, 'from the same opening', e.g. from the same crevice in the face of a rock) *sweet* (R.S.V. 'fresh') *water and bitter* (R.S.V. 'brackish').

12. Similarly, every man who stays at home and cultivates his fig-trees, his olives and his vines is aware that it is a law of nature that like produces like, that as is the root so will be the fruit. Jesus had pointed out to His disciples that grapes are not gathered from thorn-bushes nor figs from thistles (see Mt. vii. 16): so James reminds his readers that fig-trees do not yield olives or grape-vines figs.

In the same way, no one visiting salt springs such as those to be found in the vicinity of the Dead Sea would expect to discover that they were able to emit *salt water and fresh.* James does not stop to apply the moral of these simple and homely illustrations. However, in the reading followed by the A.V. in this last clause a final inference does seem to be drawn; and Hort may be right in supposing that 'the last illustration implies that not the verbal blessing of God but the cursing of men is a true index to what lies within'. It is salt water alone that is expected from these fountains, not salt water *and* fresh. The reading followed by R.V. carries on the negatives implied in the previous rhetorical questions, giving the translation 'neither can salt water yield sweet'.

c. The two wisdoms (iii. 13–18)

13. James would appear at this point to be returning, after the digression about the misuse of the tongue, to the responsibility of teachers touched upon in verse 1. A man's consciousness that he possesses the requisite wisdom for the work of a teacher and is *endued with knowledge*, expert or professional knowledge as the Greek word *epistēmōn* implies, is not in itself a sufficient qualification. Such a person must give practical *evidence* that he possesses this wisdom and understanding; and he must give it in a particular way. Just as the reality of man's faith is to be seen in the works that are its outcome, so his wisdom must be demonstrated by a *good conversation* (R.V. 'his good life'), for this is the only proof that such wisdom is something more than the product of his own egoism. The opening rhetorical question has the force of a condition, 'If there is a wise man . . .'; and the word *kalēs*, tranlasted *good*, implies that it must be obvious to others that his way of life is good (cf. 1 Pet. ii. 12 where the same expression is used).

The all-pervading characteristic of this 'good life' is meekness, a meekness that is not only wholly consistent with true wisdom but the essential accompaniment of it. Any contentiousness or arrogance, any tendency to self-assertion, any desire to glory over others is an infallible sign that the essential qualifications for a teacher are in fact lacking, for there is no *meekness of wisdom.* It is surely most significant that, when Jesus, the greatest of all Teachers, called men to Him as disciples, He bade them see that He possessed the hall-mark of the genuine teacher precisely because He was 'meek and lowly in heart' (Mt. xi. 29). And scarcely less significant is Paul's appeal to the 'meekness of Christ', when he wished to assert his authority in no uncertain manner and vindicate his behaviour as a Christian teacher and missionary (see 2 Cor. x. 1).

14. The would-be teacher should therefore look into his heart and see whether it is free from those two evils in particular which are most certain to vitiate his work,—*bitter envying* (R.V. 'bitter jealousy') *and strife* (R.V. 'faction'; R.S.V., correctly, 'selfish ambition'). The latter word, *eritheia,* was translated by Tyndale 'contention' from the Latin Vulgate. This has greatly influenced subsequent English translators. By derivation, however, the word refers, as Hort says, to 'the vice of a leader of a party created for his own pride; it is partly ambition and partly rivalry'.

The expression *glory not, and lie not against the truth* (R.S.V. 'do not boast and be false to the truth') contains the warning that, if the defects previously mentioned are present, the would-be teacher should refrain from embarking upon this work, for otherwise instead of teaching the truth he will in fact be asserting himself against others and so be false to the truth he is professing to teach. Hort brings out admirably what would appear to be the meaning of these somewhat difficult words when he says: 'The mere possession of truth is no security for true utterance of it: all utterance is so coloured by the moral and spiritual state of the speaker that truth issues as falsehood from his lips in proportion as he himself is not in a right state: the correct language which he utters may carry a message of falsehood and evil in virtue of the bitterness and self-seeking which accompanies his speaking.' Although *the truth* cannot be limited in this context to the truth of Christian revelation, the warning here given is pre-eminently relevant to the preacher of the Christian gospel. It is true that Paul on one occasion could rejoice that Christ was proclaimed even by those who had strife and envy in their hearts (see Phil. i. 15–18); but though God may have been pleased in those critical days of the Early Church to bring good out of evil, history shows that there have been many other occasions where the truth of the message has been denied by the bitterness and partisanship of the messenger.

15. Where 'bitter jealousy' and 'selfish ambition' are present in the teacher's heart, there can normally be no dissemination of true wisdom, for there is absent the fear of the Lord which is 'the beginning of wisdom'. Rather is there being manifested a counterfeit wisdom, described in this verse as descending *not from above*, i.e. not God-given; but *earthly*, owing its origin to earth-bound motives even when it is discussing heavenly things; *sensual*, i.e. conditioned and limited at all points by the unregenerate mind of man, uninfluenced by the divine Spirit (hence R.S.V. 'unspiritual'; cf. Jude 19); and *devilish*, demon-like rather than God-like, especially perhaps in its deceptiveness and its hypocrisy (see 1 Tim. iv. 1).

16. The trenchant language of the previous verse is here substantiated by the consideration that the inevitable accompaniments of jealousy and selfish ambition are the things most opposed to God's very nature and to the way of life which He desires that men should be following. 'God is not a God of confusion, but of peace' (1 Cor. xiv. 33, R.V.); but where there is 'bitter jealousy' and 'selfish ambition', there is *confusion*; the whole mental outlook is thrown into disorder, the understanding is darkened, and this spiritual instability is reflected in the instability of human society. Similarly, God is wholly antipathetic to evil; 'God is light, and in him is no darkness at all' (1 Jn. i. 5); but where there is 'bitter jealousy' and 'selfish ambition', there is *every evil work* (R.V. 'every vile deed').

17. How different from all this is *the wisdom that is from above.* In the first place, this higher wisdom is *pure* in itself, wholly free from such defilements as have been mentioned. *Then,* secondly, because of this inherent purity, it has the following beneficial characteristics. In its methods of working, and in what it achieves, it is *peaceable* and so able to promote peace between men; it is *gentle,* considerate in the demands it makes upon others; it is *easy to be intreated* (R.S.V. 'open to reason'), docile and not unwilling to yield to reasonable requests; it is *full of mercy and good fruits,* showing active sympathy towards the suffering and the sorrowing; it is *without partiality,* Gk. *adiakritos,* a difficult word which might have an active sense 'not making distinctions' as implied in A.V., or which, perhaps more probably, is used here passively in the sense of 'undivided', particularly in its allegiance to God, as implied in R.S.V. 'without uncertainty'; finally, it is *without hypocrisy* in all human relationships. This description is in full accord with the character pronounced 'blessed' by our Lord in the Beatitudes (Mt. v. 3–11) and perfectly exhibited in Himself who was the divine Wisdom incarnate.

18. James is insistent that religion must show itself in works. In this he is wholly true to his Master's words 'By their fruits ye shall know them' (Mt. vii. 20). In the expression *the fruit of righteousness* the genitive could be a genitive of origin, the fruit which is the result of righteousness and which consists of the rewards that righteous conduct brings. Not the least of such rewards is *peace,* for it is an axiom of the Bible that there can be no peace unless the claims of justice are satisfied. If this is the right exegesis, then the verse re-echoes the teaching of Is. xxxii. 17 'And the work of righteousness shall be peace; and the effect of righteousness quietness and assurance for ever'. The really blessed state is where 'righteousness and peace have kissed each other' (Ps. lxxxv. 10).

On the other hand, the genitive may be, and probably is, a genitive of definition, the fruit which consists of righteousness. In i. 20 James has stated negatively that such righteousness, the righteousness that God demands, cannot be achieved by the wrath of man. Here he asserts positively that it is the natural harvest of the seed that is *sown in peace* by *them that make peace*. This must be so, for the peace-makers are akin to God, being called His 'children' (Mt. v. 9); and God is 'the author of peace and lover of concord'.

Calvin, in an interesting comment, points out that those who exercise the wisdom that is from above, while they meekly tolerate many things in their neighbours, do not cease to sow righteousness, but strive to correct the faults of others by peaceful means. They 'moderate their zeal with the condiment of peace, for those who wish to be physicians to heal vices ought not to be executioners'!

CHAPTER IV

a. Conflict and compromise (iv. 1–10)

1. The closing verse of the previous section suggests the thought that man's ultimate good can best be described as 'peace'; and yet the most obvious feature of human life as we know it, is not peace but strife. The periods in history when nations have not been in conflict have been short; and within the nation and the family discord and faction are always lifting their ugly heads. No evidence could be more decisive than this for the truth of the Christian doctrine of original sin, which asserts that something is inherently wrong with human nature itself.

In verse 1, which consists of two rhetorical questions, James points to the source of this perpetual conflict which has such a disintegrating effect on individual personality and upon society as a whole, and is far from absent in many Christian communities. Even *among you* Christians, he implies, *wars* and *fightings* are to be found. Although what James says here about the source of conflict in human life obviously applies to war in its wider and more usual sense, and to the battles that compose it, his words in this context would appear to have a wider implication. They might perhaps be better translated 'factions' and 'quarrels'. Factions within communities are the outcome of quarrels between individuals; and both are due ultimately to the *lusts that war in your members.*

The word here translated *lusts* (*hēdonōn*) more literally means 'pleasures' (A.V. margin, R.V.). It is used in three other places in the New Testament besides the opening verses of this chapter, and always in a bad sense. In Lk. viii. 14 it is the 'pleasures of this life' which coupled with 'cares and riches' choke the seed of the divine word and prevent it from taking root in the human heart. As distinct from the ordinary Greek word meaning 'desire', *epithumia*, it means 'satisfied desire';

for pleasure lies essentially in the satisfaction of desire. A characteristic of the unredeemed life, so we read in Tit. iii. 3, is that men are in slavery to 'divers lusts and pleasures'. These pleasures, says James, *war in your members*. He does not say specifically, as Peter says of lusts (1 Pet. ii. 11), that they 'war against the soul', though that is implied; for so long as they have the upper hand man is prevented from doing what he was originally created to do—acknowledge and render obedience to the will of God. Nor does James say that these pleasures are at war with each other, as though man's main problem consisted in making a choice between higher and lower kinds of pleasure. What he asserts is that the human personality has, as it were, been invaded by an alien army which is always campaigning within it. The verb *strateuomenōn* implies that these pleasures are permanently on active service; and the expression *in your members* means that there is no part of the human frame which does not afford them a battleground. Human nature is indeed in the grip of an overwhelming army of occupation. Its natural aim, it can truthfully be said, is pleasure; and when we consider the amount of time, energy, money, interest and enthusiasm that men and women give to the satisfaction of this aim we can appreciate the accuracy of James' diagnosis; and Christians can use it as a reliable yardstick by which to measure the sincerity of their religion. Is God or pleasure the dominant concern of their life? That they will ever be free in this world from the influence of the pleasures that are at war in their members they have no right to expect; but they can be free by the grace of God from their domination.

2. In this verse James now states more specifically the direct connection that exists between pleasures and the factions and the quarrels that result from them. Commentators have always been faced with two great difficulties in this verse. The first concerns its punctuation.[1] As we read it in the A.V. there are

[1] It should be remembered that there is no punctuation or even separation of words in the ancient Greek manuscripts, so that editors are free to punctuate as they think best.

apparently three parallel clauses, though the significance of the parallelism is not at all clear.

> *Ye lust, and have not:*
> *Ye kill, and desire to have, and cannot obtain:*
> *Ye fight and war, yet ye have not, because ye ask not.*

The second difficulty lies in the words *ye kill*, which appear strange when followed immediately by *and desire*—for these would appear to create an inversion of the thought underlying the passage. It will be best to consider this difficulty first. The words *ye kill* are found in all existing Greek manuscripts and ancient versions. In spite of this, Erasmus found the difficulty of interpretation insuperable, for he assumed that the reference was to the perpetration of murder as an existing fact in the Christian communities known to the author. He therefore suggested the emendation 'Ye envy'. The two verbs in Greek meaning 'murder', *phoneuete*, and 'envy', *phthoneite*, are not sufficiently dissimilar for any assumption that such a change between them could not have taken place in the course of textual transmission; and it is interesting to notice that in 1 Pet. ii. 1 the fourth-century Codex Vaticanus confuses the cognate nouns and reads 'murders' for 'envyings'. The text of the New Testament has, however, been so well preserved that resort to emendation should not be made. This particular emendation commended itself nevertheless to Tyndale, who translated 'Ye envy and have indignation and cannot obtain', and to Calvin and others, including in our day James Moffatt.

There is, however, no overwhelming difficulty in the words *ye kill*, provided that the punctuation is adopted which was suggested by Westcott and Hort in the margin of their Greek Testament published in 1881, and has commended itself increasingly to modern translators and commentators. The nature and significance of this revised punctuation can perhaps best be seen in the translation of the R.S.V.

> 'You desire and do not have; so you kill.
> And you covet and cannot obtain; so you fight and wage war.'

Here we have a genuine parallelism in spite of the presence of 'and' before 'you covet'; and the consequences to which thwarted desire and unsatisfied covetousness lead are clearly brought out. Though each clause is in the nature of a statement, the verbs being in the indicative, the sentences are virtually conditional. 'If you desire . . . the result is you kill. And if you covet . . . the result is you fight and wage war.'

James, we must not forget, is writing a general Epistle, and is not necessarily contemplating either here, or elsewhere, the circumstances actually existing in a particular Christian community known to him. He is rather underlining what *can* happen and *does* happen in human life when men choose pleasure to the exclusion of God. Under such circumstances, as the history of humanity from the days of Cain to the present time makes abundantly clear, the laws of God are disregarded; and pleasure, given full rein, takes control of the situation and often sweeps its victims on to murder. The story of Naboth's vineyard is the classic example in the Old Testament of the mighty power of covetousness and of the end to which it can lead.

The Greek words translated *Ye lust*, *epithumeite*, and *Ye desire to have*, *zēloute*, do not have quite the same meaning. The former is sometimes used in a bad sense, as here, of desiring passionately, or coveting, something that belongs to another (as in Acts xx. 33; Mt. v. 28); while the latter is used both in the good sense of burning with zeal, or in the bad sense of burning with envy (as in Acts vii. 9, xvii. 5; 1 Cor. xiii. 4; Gal. iv. 17). Hort, perhaps rightly, considered that the latter word in the present context expresses 'envy of position or rank or fame . . . sordid and bitter personal ambition'. There are indeed few evils in human life that cannot be traced to covetousness and envy in the sense in which we find these words used in this verse. Covetousness does not always lead to possession, envy does not always attain to the position of its rivals—and the inevitable result is conflict and strife.

The word *yet* before *ye have not* is omitted by the best ancient authorities, and the last words of the verse should be taken as a separate clause *ye have not because ye ask not*. The thought behind them seems to be that men and women can obtain *real* satisfaction only by praying to Him who alone can give it.

As long as they allow their lives to be governed by pleasure, real satisfaction, consisting of true peace, full contentment, and solid joy, will always be beyond their reach. Man's primary need, therefore, is to desire the right things; i.e. the things that God will bestow upon His children if they ask Him for them, just because He knows that they will promote their highest welfare. There is, to be sure, no prayer that we all need to pray so much as the prayer that we may *love* what God commands and *desire* what He promises.

3. Here we find a small qualification of the somewhat sweeping negative of the previous clause. James is writing to *Christians*, even though they are Christians who are far from being wholly God-centred; and he reminds them that those whose lives are either completely under the control of pleasures, as is the case with the unregenerate, or who still feel the pressure of such pleasures as a disintegrating factor in their lives, even though they be regenerate, *may* offer prayers, but their prayers are not likely to be such as God will listen to. The reason is that their ulterior motive is that they may have more time, better health and increased strength to spend in the satisfaction of their own desires. *So* to pray is to *ask amiss*. The R.V. translation 'spend it in your pleasures' is preferable.

The Bible makes it perfectly clear whose prayers God is ready to accept. His ears are open to the cries of the righteous (Ps. xxxiv. 15). He is nigh unto all that call upon Him in truth (Ps. cxlv. 18). He listens to the penitent (Lk. xviii. 14). And He hears all who ask anything that is according to His will (1 Jn. v. 14). The prayers of all such ascend directly to the throne of grace.

4. If we accept the reading *ye adulterers and adulteresses*, we should probably interpret the expression literally, and suppose that this particular category of sinners is selected by the author as the one in which 'friendship with the world' is most conspicuously illustrated. The words *Ye adulterers and* are not, however, found in the most ancient Greek manuscripts of the Epistle, nor in the ancient versions. It is therefore most probable that they were inserted later, when *adulteresses* was interpreted literally and it seemed natural that their masculine counterparts should also be mentioned. We should interpret the expression metaphorically. Our Lord called the generation He had come to serve an 'adulterous generation' because it was disloyal and unfaithful (Mt. xii. 39). Refusing to see the obvious signs of God's love manifest in the works of Jesus, it demanded a special sign. The disloyalty of Israel to God was often designated 'adultery' by the prophets; and the feminine word used by James suggests that he had especially in mind the wantonness of Hosea's wife, in whose unfaithfulness the prophet was bidden to see an acted parable of the unfaithfulness of God's people. In the same sense, worldly-minded Christians are *adulteresses*. In modern English it would be better perhaps to translate by some such expression as 'unfaithful creatures' (R.S.V.). Just as God in the Old Testament is constantly depicted as the husband of Israel, so Christ was thought of by the early Christians as the heavenly Bridegroom and the Church His Bride.

The Church as a whole, or individual Christians in particular, are unfaithful to Christ when they show 'friendship with the world' (R.S.V.). This translation brings out better than *the friendship of the world* (A.V.) the force of the objective genitive. The Christian cannot, without compromising his position, divide his affection between God and those forces in the world which show either complete indifference to God or are openly hostile to Him. Similarly, selfishness in any form, whether it be the love of pleasure, self-gratification or arrogant self-seeking, is all 'friendship with the world'; and for the time being it causes the Christian to be at war with God, though God's attitude to him remains one of Fatherly love. He remains faithful. Sometimes the expulsive power of a new affection is so evident in the Christian convert, and love for God becomes so much the dominating factor in his life, that any compromise with the moral standards of the world is almost unthinkable. In others sin still remains very active, even after conversion, and the task of living in the world and yet not of it is much more difficult. James' reminder that friendship with the world involves enmity with God puts into different language the decisive words of Jesus to His disciples, 'Ye cannot serve God and mammon' (Mt. vi. 24); while the implied corollary that love of God will involve for the Christian the world's hatred echoes the warning of Jesus to His followers 'because ye are not of the world . . . therefore the world hateth you' (Jn. xv. 19).

It should be noted that the text emphasizes the truth that it is the *deliberate choice* by the Christian of worldly conduct which constitutes him an enemy of God. It may often be that the Christian finds himself quite unwillingly in an atmosphere pervaded by worldly standards. He cannot help being where he is. James is saying that to seek out such company of set purpose is like walking over into the enemy's camp. This truth is better brought out in the translation, 'Whoever wishes to be a friend of the world makes himself an enemy of God' (R.S.V.).

5. The interpretation of this verse has always been found difficult. It will be best to consider first the meaning of the words which are presented as being a quotation from Scripture. Tyndale, following the reading found in the mass of late manuscripts, 'which dwelleth in you', translated: 'The spirit that dwelleth in you lusteth even contrary to envy but giveth more grace'; and in the margin he commented: 'Christ's spirit (which is in all that be His, Rom. viii) resisteth hate envy and all sin. Whose motion if one follow, grace increaseth in us and lusts minish and therefore He says Submit yourselves to God, etc.' It is clear that Tyndale took the Greek preposition *to* as meaning here 'contrary to', which should be *para* and not *pros*, and *envy* as human envy; and that he connected the sentence with verse 8 rather than with verse 4. A.V. does not follow Tyndale, but refers 'envy' to divine envy and translates *The spirit that dwelleth in us lusteth to envy.* R.V., in the text, follows A.V. except that it adopts the reading found in the most ancient Greek MSS. 'which he made to dwell', and, turning the quotation into a separate question, translates, 'Doth the spirit which he made to dwell in us long unto envying?', to which it would seem, the answer 'No' is expected. The

Revisers, however, were aware that the clause could be a statement and not a question; that the subject of the principal verb could be 'God' and not 'the spirit'; and that 'the spirit' could be its object. Hence the marginal rendering 'The spirit which he made to dwell in us he yearneth for even unto jealous envy'. R.S.V. has rightly followed this R.V. marginal rendering, and, incorporating the words into the previous question, translates 'Or do you suppose it is in vain that the scripture says, "He yearns jealously over the spirit which he has made to dwell in us"?'

This verse, in effect, gives the reader scriptural authority for what has been stated in verse 4 about the incompatibility of friendship of the world and friendship of God. God is a jealous God who will brook no rivals. It is His Spirit that has been given to the Christian, and He cannot view with anything but jealousy the harbouring by the Christian within his soul of any rival spirit such as the spirit of the world. It is true that there is no passage in the Old Testament which exactly corresponds to these words. Rather do they sum up the content of many passages.[1] But where sin abounds, grace more than abounds; and God in His love does not abandon the Christian in his temporary unfaithfulness, but His grace is always available for him in time of need. God's demand for undivided allegiance goes hand in hand with His supply of the divine aid necessary for rendering that allegiance. *He giveth more grace.*

6. This axiom of the divine working—that the greater His people's needs the greater is God's supply of the requisite grace—underlies the quotation from Pr. iii. 34 made in this verse, and found also in 1 Pet. v. 5. *The proud* are those whose hearts are turned away from their Creator and who set themselves up against all that is holy or called God. Such pride expresses itself especially in a contempt for God's servants. To all such God is permanently opposed. He actively resists them. His wrath abides upon them. On the contrary *the humble* are those who recognize their insufficiency, are conscious of their creaturely estate and absolute dependence upon Almighty

[1] See additional note on *The jealousy of God*, p. 105.

God, and are willing to receive from Him and Him alone all that is necessary for their salvation. It is assumed by James that Christians, however great may be their temporary backslidings, are fundamentally humble in this sense, and that therefore they are the fitting recipients of the grace which God is ready to bestow upon all that are of a meek and contrite spirit. For, as we read in Job, 'When men are cast down, then thou shalt say, There is lifting up; and he shall save the humble person' (Jb. xxii. 29).

7. Not unnaturally James passes from the statement that it is the humble whose hearts are open to receive God's grace to the injunction to his readers *submit yourselves to God.* For the readiness to submit ourselves to others is a characteristic of humility. We can *obey* others without any humility, acting either under compulsion or from motives of expediency; but we can only *submit ourselves* to others when we recognize that they are greater, better, or more worthy of honour than ourselves. Submission to others, whether it be as citizens to magistrates in the legitimate discharge of their duties, or as wives to husbands, or as slaves to masters, or as children to parents is enjoined in the New Testament as a paramount Christian duty. It is, however, transformed into something richer and better than mere duty when it is done 'for the Lord's sake' (see 1 Pet. ii. 13) and as a natural outcome of that total submission which the Christian renders to God alone. Submission to God and the possession of a truly humble spirit cannot in fact be separated.

Because pride separates a man from God more than anything else, and prevents that perfect submission to Him which is the essential pre-requisite for receiving His blessings, James very naturally follows the call for submission with the command *Resist the devil.* In effect this imperative has a conditional force, the sense being 'If you resist the devil, he will flee from you'. The devil knows well enough that his greatest hope of drawing Christians away from a whole-hearted and voluntary submission to God lies in appealing to their wounded pride. Paul was well aware of his tactics. Hence his injunction that positions of authority in the Church should not be occupied by a novice lest being lifted up with pride he fall into the condemnation of the devil (1 Tim. iii. 6).

The devil is constantly saying to the Christian 'Why keep so closely to the narrow way and the humble path? Why not be more self-assertive? Why not express yourself as fully as you can, and find power and enjoyment in that self-expression? I am the prince of the world and the whole world lies under me (see Jn. xiv. 30; 1 Jn. v. 19). I offer you to the full the pleasures and the happiness of the world.' So the Christ Himself was tempted in the wilderness at the beginning of His ministry, and also later again when the seeds of civil rebellion sprang to life in the hearts of the ever restless Galileans, after He had lavished upon them His royal bounty, and they tried to make Him an earthly king. But each time He resisted the devil; on the former occasion (Mt. iv. 8–10) by a weapon drawn from the armoury of holy Scripture, and on the latter by withdrawing to the hills to be alone in prayer to His heavenly Father (Jn. vi. 15). As Christ resisted the evil one, so too must His subjects; and we are assured here that our very resistance will constitute our victory. We *can* resist because we have been born again as children of God and have the weapon of faith as our shield (see 1 Jn. v. 18; Eph. vi. 16; 1 Pet. v. 8).

8. The opening sentence of verse 8 provides both a parallel and a contrast to the last half of verse 7. Resistance to the devil, when he approaches the Christian to try and deflect him from serving the Lord, results in the flight of the devil; but, when the Christian wills to come close to God, God comes close to him. Those who approach God most frequently live closest to Him and therefore find it easiest to offer resistance to the devil. The right to draw near to God and the knowledge that God is near to them are the characteristics which most distinguish God's people from other nations of the world. 'For what great nation is there, that hath God so nigh unto them, as the Lord our God is whensoever we call upon him?' (Dt. iv. 7, R.V.). Under the old dispensation, it was the special function of the priests to come near to God (see Ex. xix. 22) at set times and offer sacrifice on behalf of the people. Under the new dispensation, the privilege is open to all believers. They can approach boldly to the throne of grace at any time. Nor need they come with hands laden with sacrificial gifts, for they have only to plead the shed blood of Jesus (see Heb. iv. 16).

Cleanse your hands. Under the old covenant, washing of hands was a ritual duty laid especially upon the priests as part of the process by which they were rendered fit to perform their ceremonial duties (see Ex. xxx. 20). This was one of the means by which mankind was taught the great lesson of the holiness of God. Under the influence of scribal tradition ceremonial washing of hands at the time of our Lord was widely practised and not confined to any one section of the community (cf. Mk. vii. 3, 4). From these ceremonial uses the expression came very naturally to be applied figuratively to the removal of moral defilement. Christians are constantly stained by such defilement. Though no longer under the dominion of sin they commit sin; and if they deny this fact they are self-deceived (see 1 Jn. i. 8). James does not hesitate, therefore, to use the word *sinners* even though he is addressing Christians and to remind them to cleanse their hands, i.e. to repent, for he assumes that they know that the blood of Jesus Christ cleanseth us from *all* sin (see 1 Jn. i. 7). The word *sinners*, so often associated in the Gospels with 'tax-collectors', was used by the Pharisees to describe all who either could not, or would not, keep the ceremonial laws and traditions of the elders. Here it is used of Christians who fail by sins of commission or omission to fulfil the law of Christ.

The influence of the world as it organizes itself apart from God presses so strongly upon the Christian that it is very difficult for him to avoid entirely those moral defilements which render him a sinner. Under such influences his mind and affections are torn very often in two different directions. In Paul's language, the good that he would he does not, but the evil which he would not he does (see Rom. vii. 19). He thus becomes *double minded*, wavering in his loyalties, undecided in his intentions, divided in his interests, and, as a result, lacks that purity of heart and singleness of purpose which our Lord expects in His disciples. This is a most dangerous condition; and the remedy for it is a re-dedication of the whole personality to Christ and a fresh submission to the cleansing power of the Holy Spirit. The word *purify*, *hagnisate*, often used in the Bible with a ceremonial meaning (e.g. Jn. xi. 55), is used by Peter to describe the purification of the soul which results from the initial obedience to the truth of the gospel (1 Pet. i. 22), and also by James in this verse and by John in 1 Jn. iii. 3 to remind their Christian readers that the whole life of the Christian must be one of constant purification under the power of the divine Spirit.

9. When the Christian compromises with the world and is *double minded*, it is a sure sign that his sense of the gravity of sin has become blunted. Accordingly in this verse James recalls his readers to that sober earnestness which is the proper demeanour of a Christian when faced with the reality of sin. Vapid hilarity, false heartiness, unseemly gaiety, a light and frivolous spirit—these are wholly out of place in the life of a converted man or woman. There is, it is true, a Christian joy of which no man can rob its possessors. It is to be found in believing the good news of the redemption achieved by Jesus; it can be experienced in the thrill of conflict as the Christian struggles against temptation; it is inherent in the happiness of service rendered to those for whom Christ died; and it is present even when he is suffering persecution for the Master's sake. So long, however, as sin is active in the believer's own life and is working its havoc in the lives of others, the mourning of penitence and the sorrow of sympathy must be among the Christian's most deeply felt emotions. Jesus, sinless Himself, felt so keenly the burden of the world's sin that we are perhaps not surprised to find that, while there is mention in the Gospels of His tears, there is no record of His laughter. He wept at the grave of His friend Lazarus, when the horror of the death which sin brings in its train seems to have been borne in upon Him with special intensity causing Him acute disturbance of spirit (Jn. xi. 33); He wept again, as He approached Jerusalem, and saw the holy city lying at His feet with its magnificent buildings bathed in the spring sunshine but with its inhabitants unconscious of the doom which their disobedience to God's will was so inevitably and so speedily to bring upon them (Lk. xix. 41); and He bade the women of Jerusalem on the way to Calvary stop weeping for Him but rather weep for themselves and their children in view of all that was coming upon them (Lk. xxiii. 28).

How natural, then, that James should remind his readers, many of whom were in danger of becoming friends of the world and *double minded*, that affliction, mourning, and weeping, all of which are experienced by every man and woman in times of sorrow, pain, disappointment and bereavement, must be in a real sense permanent characteristics of the Christian. When he bids them *Be afflicted*, he is not urging them to lay upon themselves self-inflicted hardships as acts of penance which will merit their salvation; but rather to experience that sense of wretchedness (R.S.V.) from which no one who is really sensitive to the burden of the world's sin can ever be free, and that godly sorrow which leads to repentance (see 2 Cor. vii. 10). Paul, for all the joy that he experienced as a Christian, cried out 'O wretched man that I am!' (Rom. vii. 24); and the adjective he uses of himself is cognate to the verb *talaipōrēsate* used here by James.

James bids his readers of their own accord abandon all light-hearted *laughter* for the *mourning* which Jesus describes as an essential ingredient of the blessed life (Mt. v. 4), and to substitute for joy, *heaviness* or 'dejection' (R.S.V.). The latter word *katēpheia* means, by derivation, a downcast look; such a look is characteristic of the true penitent, as Jesus taught when He said about the publican in His parable, he 'would not lift up so much as his eyes unto heaven, but smote upon his breast, saying, God be merciful to me a sinner' (Lk. xviii. 13). The Bible recognizes laughter as one of the great gifts of God. In it we read that God fills the mouth of the perfect man with laughter (Jb. viii. 21). But the Bible also recognizes that there is a laughter born of flippancy, scorn and self-satisfaction. Sarah's laughter on hearing the divine promise that she should become the mother of Abraham's children was unseemly because it reflected a failure to appreciate the omnipotency of God (see Gn. xviii. 12, 13). Similarly, Jesus pronounced a woe upon those whose laughter revealed an ignorance of their own true condition and status before God (Lk. vi. 25). Like the church of the Laodiceans they knew not that they were 'wretched, and miserable, and poor, and blind, and naked' (Rev. iii. 17). Only when they accepted the invitation to *mourn and weep* would they enjoy the blessedness of the kingdom of God and laugh with a holy, guileless, laughter in the company of the saints.

10. It is only as men and women attempt to see themselves *in the sight of the Lord*, i.e. as God sees them, that they can view themselves in true perspective. If they form their own opinions of themselves, or are content with the judgments of their fellows about themselves, the result will almost certainly be either unduly flattering or unduly depreciatory. It is only when we see ourselves by the aid of the Holy Spirit against the background of the revelation of God contained in the Bible that our judgment is right. And, when this task is faithfully undertaken, we are forced to acknowledge our littleness and our unworthiness. We are humbled in the sight of God. But such a sense of humiliation, so far from being a cause of despair, is the essential condition of our exaltation. James accordingly ends this present series of exhortations to his readers by the injunction which picks up the dominant thought of verse 6, *Humble yourselves in the sight of the Lord*; and he assures them that exaltation will most certainly follow. Such exaltation is for the Christian both an immediate and a more distant reality. All who submit to the will of God, at any stage in their spiritual pilgrimage, are *ipso facto* exalted. Because Mary expressed her complete obedience in the words 'Behold the handmaid of the Lord; be it unto me according to thy word', and by so doing placed herself among the noble company of those who humble themselves before God, she could rejoice that the Lord had already uplifted her. Hence the exalted strains of her *Magnificat*. Yet the humble servants of God will find their exaltation complete only when they reign with Christ in glory. Meanwhile they have the promise of Jesus recorded on more than one occasion in the Gospels that 'he that shall humble himself shall be exalted' (Mt. xxiii. 12; Lk. xiv. 11, xviii. 14). Calvin in commenting on this verse quotes a pertinent saying of Augustine: 'As a tree must strike deep roots downwards, that it may grow upwards, so every one who has not his soul fixed deep in humility, exalts himself to his own ruin'.

b. Backbiting and judging (iv. 11, 12)

11. The verb translated in the A.V. *speak not evil*, *katalaleite*, means literally 'talk another down', or 'talk against another'. Hence the R.V. rendering here, 'Speak not one against another'. In later Greek the word seems to have had the additional significance of speaking about others behind their backs in a derogatory manner. It is found with this sense in the Septuagint version of Ps. ci. 5, translated in the A.V. 'Whoso privily slandereth his neighbour', and of Ps. l. 20, translated 'Thou sittest and speakest against thy brother; thou slanderest thine own mother's son'. It is therefore probable that the word has this implication in this present verse also, and that Tyndale was right in translating 'backbite'. The corresponding adjective in Rom. i. 30 is rendered 'backbiters' in both the A.V. and the R.V. It is interesting to notice that in this verse from James the R.S.V. has returned to the A.V. and translates 'Do not speak evil against one another'.

In the Christian Church believers are bound to one another spiritually with as close a tie as that which physically binds brothers together in a human family. It is to be noticed therefore that James makes a special appeal to his readers at this point by addressing them as *brethren*; and he repeats the word 'brother' twice in the following sentence. To defame, slander or malign a fellow-member of the body of Christ is as infamous as 'to slander thine own mother's son'.

It is not certain whether this brief section is connected closely in thought with verse 10, or has a more general reference to the theme of the previous section as a whole. If the former interpretation is right, backbiting is taken as a signal illustration of the failure to possess that humility which alone makes it possible for anyone to be exalted by the Lord. It is indeed very true that those who indulge in the habit of running down their neighbours, or a fellow-member of their church, often do so because they feel that, in so doing, they are implying that they themselves are very much better people than those they disparage. Backbiting others is, in fact, a subtle form of self-exaltation. As Calvin comments: 'Hypocrisy is always presumptuous, and we are by nature hypocrites, fondly exalting ourselves by calumniating others.' If, however, the connection is with the previous section as a whole, the writer would appear to be illustrating the Christian's danger of compromising with the world by emphasizing a sphere of conduct where he is most liable to be tempted: for how large a part of 'worldly' talk, which often passes as witty and is far from being unacceptable to society, consists of harsh criticism of other people, spoken sometimes with malicious intent, and sometimes with a thoughtlessness no less cruel because unintentional and devoid of any understanding of the harm that is being done. It would indeed be difficult to estimate how many friendships are broken, how many reputations ruined, and the peace of how many homes destroyed through careless gossip often indulged in for the lack of something better to do!

The A.V. follows the mass of late manuscripts in reading *and judgeth*. The R.V. reverts to the reading of the more ancient manuscripts, 'or judgeth'. It may very well be that the A.V. rendering best interprets the sense. Backbiting and judging a brother are not put forward as alternatives. In the process of backbiting, James seems to suggest, the slanderer is in fact passing judgment. In doing this he is going far beyond the bounds of what is legitimate for ordinary human beings. In a human court of law, it is true, the judge is bound to pass judgment, but only in the light of specific charges and after all the facts have been discovered as far as it is humanly possible to discover them. The backbiter, on the other hand, is in effect passing judgment without either the opportunity of knowing, or, it may be, without even the desire to know the truth.

He that speaketh evil of his brother is in fact so lacking in humility that he is behaving as though the divine prerogative of judgment had been assigned to him. He is, moreover, as James goes on to say, not only speaking evil of his *brother* and judging his *brother*. He also *speaketh evil of the law, and judgeth the law*. Although there is no definite article before 'law' in the original, it is clear that it is the divine law which is here in question, and not law in general. It may be that James has in mind the specific indictment of backbiting found in Lv. xix. 16 where it is written, 'Thou shalt not go up and down as a talebearer among thy people' or the more general law referred to in ii. 8 as 'the royal law according to the scripture, Thou shalt love thy neighbour as thyself'. In any case, the former command is an essential part of the latter, as the context in Leviticus makes clear, for the words 'Thou shalt not bear any grudge against the children of thy people' are followed by 'but thou shalt love thy neighbour as thyself' (Lv. xix. 18). By violating this royal law the backbiter is in effect passing judgment upon it. For, as Mayor well comments, 'whoever deliberately breaks a law and does not repent of it, thereby speaks evil against it and treats it as a bad law, since it is the essence of a law to require obedience, and he who refuses obedience virtually says it ought not to be law'. Man's duty is to carry out what God commands, and not to sit in judgment upon it; and to obey, even when the full reason for what is commanded may not be clear, though, to be sure, the evils of backbiting are so self-evident that it is a mark of crass and wilful stupidity to fail to recognize them. When man ceases to be a *doer of the law*, he becomes *ipso facto a judge*, such a judge, James implies, as God and only God can be, for He alone is not under law. Of no one else can it be stated as an ultimate truth that he is a law to himself.

12. In this verse James does not mean to suggest that there are not, or ought not to be any human legislators. What he is emphasizing is that there is only *one lawgiver* whose laws are of permanent significance and whose judgments are of eternal validity, for there is only One who is Lord of life and death, *who is able to save and to destroy*. James is here reiterating the great truth about the divine nature revealed to Moses in the words 'I kill, and I make alive . . . neither is there any that can deliver out of my hand' (Dt. xxxii. 39). Of all the lawgivers in the world God alone is strong enough and competent enough to detect, convict, and punish *all* who disregard or disobey His enactments. Jesus told His disciples that God was to be feared precisely for this reason. 'I say unto you my friends, Be not afraid of them that kill the body, and after that have no more that they can do. But I will forewarn you whom ye shall fear: Fear him, which after he hath killed hath power to cast into hell; yea, I say unto you, Fear him' (Lk. xii. 4, 5). How infinitely pathetic, how rashly presumptuous, and how utterly futile it is for weak, incompetent man to try and take it upon himself to judge his neighbours. As Paul wrote of the superior Jew who sought to pass judgment upon the Gentile, 'wherein thou judgest another, thou condemnest thyself' (Rom. ii. 1). '*Who art thou*', James asks, and the emphasis in the original on the personal pronoun makes his question one of profound scorn, '*who art thou that judgest another?*'

c. Presumptuous confidence (iv. 13–17)

13. As another example, held up for the warning of Christians, of the worldliness which causes its victims to neglect God and to arrange their lives as though He did not exist and as if they alone were masters of their destiny, James apostrophizes the self-confident travelling traders, probably Jews, with whom his readers would be familiar. The interjection *Go to now* arrests the reader's attention; and is loosely but not wrongly translated into the Latin versions by *ecce*, 'behold'. The following words, which James puts into the mouth of an imaginary group of itinerant merchants as they draw up their plans for the immediate future, express their unqualified confidence that that future is in their own keeping. The exact day of their departure, *To day or to morrow*, or, if we adopt the variant reading *To day and to morrow*, the precise time the contemplated journey will take; the particular city they will visit, *such a city* (perhaps pointing it out to one another on the map); the length of their proposed stay in it, *a year*; the business that they intend to transact; and the profit they assume will result from their bargaining;—all these matters, they take it for granted, are their concern and no one else's. *We will go . . . , and continue there . . . , and buy and sell, and get gain.*

Such presumptuous confidence about the future is denounced in no uncertain terms in Pr. xxvii. 1, 'Boast not thyself of to morrow; for thou knowest not what a day may bring forth', a passage which James may well have had in mind when he wrote this verse. It also forms the theme of what is perhaps the most satirical of our Lord's parables, that of the rich fool, who in making his plans for his future security forgot that the tenure of his life was something that it was not in his power to determine, and who found to his dismay that the moment when those plans seemed complete was the precise moment when he would no longer be there to benefit from them (Lk. xii. 16–21).

14. The radical fault with such people, James goes on to assert, is that they are making an entirely false classification of themselves. The words *Whereas ye know not what shall be on the morrow* mean, more exactly, 'seeing that you are of such a nature that you are ignorant of what shall be on the morrow'. In other words, they forget that they are human creatures and no more. They are not even prophets specially endowed with the power of foretelling what God would have men know about the future. For them, as for all other ordinary mortals, that future must remain uncertain and undefined.

Equally serious is their failure to recognize their frailty and the transience of their existence. So James challenges them with the abrupt but arresting question, *What is your life?* There is no *for* in the original; and the word *what*, *poia*, means 'of what character?' They fondly suppose that their life is secure, a solid substantial thing that will stand four-square against the winds of circumstance. In fact, *it is even a vapour, that appeareth for a little time, and then vanisheth away*. The only certain factor about human life is that it will end sooner or later in death; and the refusal to face up to the inevitableness of death, or the failure to remember that it may come at a time unexpected and in a manner unforeseen, is a sign of human arrogance. The R.V., followed by the R.S.V., adopts the alternative reading, 'Ye are a vapour'. As it is human beings that are seen, if only for a brief space, rather than life itself, this may perhaps be original.

The nearest parallel to this description of human life as vapour is to be found in Wisdom ii. 4, where the godless, recognizing that their life 'shall pass away as the trace of a cloud, and shall be dispersed as a mist, that is driven away with the beams of the sun', decide to adopt a purely hedonistic attitude to life. James, on the other hand, uses the same consideration of the uncertainty of life's duration to call his readers to a greater sense of their absolute dependence upon Almighty God.

15. The words *For that ye ought to say* are to be connected with *ye that say* in verse 13. What men and women ought always to be saying in their hearts, and sometimes to be uttering with their lips, are the words, *If the Lord will, we shall live, and do this, or that.* Both life itself and what we are able to do with it depend on the divine will. Providence cannot be neglected and it cannot be defeated. It is interesting to notice that the A.V. does not follow here the text of Erasmus accepted by Tyndale, which is also the text of the Latin Vulgate, 'If the Lord will and we live, we shall do this or that'. This reading is inferior because it does not bring out so clearly as the other the important truth, so strongly stressed in this passage, that we are dependent upon God for life itself.

No one was more conscious of the reality of providence than the apostle Paul. It is not therefore surprising that we often find him giving expression to it as he looks towards the future. When he bade the Christians at Ephesus farewell, he said, 'I will return again unto you, if God will' (Acts xviii. 21). His decision to visit the Corinthians in the near future is qualified in 1 Corinthians by the provisos 'if the Lord will' and 'if the Lord permit' (1 Cor. iv. 19, xvi. 7). He 'trusts in the Lord Jesus' that he will be able to send Timothy shortly to the

Philippians, and that he himself will also be able to pay them a visit (Phil. ii. 19, 24).

There is a real danger that the expression 'God willing', so often and so sincerely used by Christians in days when the sovereignty of God was a deep reality to them, and still more the expression *deo volente* in its shortened form 'd.v.', may be used too glibly and so become a formality devoid of religious content. For the most part, however, Christians today do not give sufficient expression to this sense of man's utter dependence upon the will of the transcendent God; and they might profitably ask themselves whether their refusal to say 'God willing' is really due to a horror of hypocrisy or to a failure to acknowledge the supremacy of God.

16. *But now*, James goes on to say to the proud traders he has been describing, 'so far from making it clear by what you say that you recognize your dependence upon God, you actually *rejoice in your boastings*'. In other words, their arrogant speeches are expressions of self-glorification and of the joy they find in imagining they have power to control their own destiny. The word translated *boastings*, *alazoniais*, by its derivation suggests the thought that these people are wandering in an unreal world of speculation and boasting to others about what they think they have found there! The word is found once again in the New Testament, in the expression 'the pride of life' (see 1 Jn. ii. 16). *All such rejoicing* (R.V. 'glorying') *is evil.* Other rejoicings and gloryings may be legitimate but *such* rejoicing as this can be described only as *evil.*

17. James sums up this section with a maxim which has wider inferences for Christians than that which is drawn from it in this particular context.[1] What he has written in the preceding verses he wishes his readers to regard chiefly as a warning against presumptuous self-confidence, and as a reminder of their duty 'to walk humbly with their God'. Such humility is a divine requirement (see Mi. vi. 8); and to know of this requirement but in practice to ignore it constitutes in itself sin.

[1] See the additional note on *Sins of Omission*, p. 106.

Additional note: The jealousy of God (iv. 5)

That God is a jealous God is an axiom of the Old Testament. In Ex. xxxiv. 14 it is stated that His 'name is Jealous'; and His jealousy is said in the second commandment (Ex. xx. 5) to be the reason why men are forbidden to make any likeness or image of God upon earth; such an image is bound to become an object of worship, and God must either be worshipped exclusively or not at all. Whenever Israel tried to combine the worship of the true God with other deities the comment of the Bible is such as we read in Dt. xxxii. 16, 'They provoked him to jealousy with strange gods, with abominations provoked they him to anger'. Throughout the Old Testament God is so concerned for the undivided allegiance and service of His own chosen people that the prophet can write, 'Thus saith the Lord of hosts; I was jealous for Zion with great jealousy, and I was jealous for her with great fury' (Zc. viii. 2).

It is a sign of the extent to which many in the modern world have lost the conception of the sovereignty of God that the idea of God's jealousy should be resented as attributing to God a characteristic which is said to be unworthy of His nature. When the ten commandments are recited in some churches there is apt to be a significant omission of the last half of the second! It is true that such a specific mention of the divine jealousy as we find in Jas. iv. 5 is unique in the New Testament; but many of the characteristics of God so clearly displayed in the Old Testament are assumed by the writers of the New Testament; and further revelation necessitated fresh emphasis but not an abandonment of previous conceptions. Yet Paul does not hesitate to challenge the Corinthians, at a time when they were tending to think that idolatry in any form was for them beyond the bounds of possibility, with the arresting question 'Do we provoke the Lord to jealousy? are we stronger than he?' (1 Cor. x. 22). It is true also that the word used for jealousy in Jas. iv. 5, *phthonos*, when it is applied to human beings, usually denotes the malicious ill-will often felt by men and women towards those who are more fortunate or successful than themselves. It should, however, be remembered that the Bible, containing as it does a revelation of God to men in terms intelligible to men, is bound to speak anthropomorphically. Love, hate, anger, jealousy are all human words, yet all of them can have and do have a transcendental meaning when applied to the sovereign God.

With regard to jealousy, we should not forget that, even as a trait of unredeemed human nature, it is not always evil. Petty jealousy and spiteful envy do indeed spoil human life. Yet a husband and wife who felt no jealousy at the intrusion of a lover or an adulterer into their home would surely be lacking in moral perception; for the exclusiveness of marriage is of the essence of marriage. It is surely not without significance that the jealousy of God mentioned in Jas. iv. 5 reflects most directly the Old Testament revelation of the marital relationship between God and His people such as is portrayed particularly in Jeremiah and Hosea. As God performs all the duties of a true and faithful husband, so He demands love and chastity from His people; and when He rebukes Israel for apostasy He complains that they have polluted themselves with adultery. It is interesting to notice that Calvin in his exposition of the second commandment associates almost exclusively the jealousy of God with the marital relationship between God and His people. 'Therefore, as the purer and chaster the husband is, the more grievously he is offended when he sees his wife inclining to a rival; so the Lord, who has betrothed us to Himself in truth, declares that He burns with the hottest jealousy, whenever, neglecting the purity of His holy marriage, we defile ourselves with abominable lusts, and especially when the worship of His deity, which ought to have been most carefully kept unimpaired, is transferred to another, or adulterated with some superstition; since, in this way, we not only violate our plighted troth, but defile the nuptial couch, by giving access to adulterers.'[1]

Additional note: Sins of omission (iv. 17)

The only specific definition of sin in the New Testament is found in 1 Jn. iii. 4, 'Sin is lawlessness'. This can imply either

[1] *Institutes of the Christian Religion*, Book II, chapter viii.

that 'sin is the transgression of the law', as the A.V. translates, or that sin is a failure to do what the law demands. It is this latter aspect of sin that finds expression in the succinct maxim found in Jas. iv. 17 *To him that knoweth to do good, and doeth it not, to him it is sin.* The teaching of James at this point is very much in keeping with the teaching of Jesus which is contained in many of His parables, where the emphasis is laid upon the sinfulness not so much of positive wrong-doing as of a failure to do right. Often the severity of His censure seems to fall upon sins of omission.

In the parable of the talents, the man who received the one talent is strongly condemned, not because he had done any definite wrong, but because he had buried a precious gift, treating it as a dead and ugly thing, when in fact it was something living and capable of being productive. He had not used it for any evil purpose, but he had done no good with it. Similarly, in the story of the Good Samaritan, the priest and Levite are mentioned with obvious contempt not because they had violated any detailed commandment, but because they were so preoccupied with their ecclesiastical business that they failed to respond to the call of human need. They were guilty of no direct breach of law, but had missed the opportunity of doing good by showing mercy to one who needed it. In the parable of the rich man and Lazarus, the former finds himself in torment in the life beyond the grave, not because he has been rich, but because he had yielded to the temptation, which especially besets the wealthy, to use his wealth to screen himself from any personal contact with those whom he found uncongenial or who lived in circumstances more humble than his own. As a result, he failed to recognize and use opportunities of service which lay at his very doorstep. He created a gulf between Lazarus and himself; and that gulf remained fixed after they were parted by death.

Nor should we forget in this connection the parable of the last assize, with which the main teaching of Jesus, as it is found in the Gospel of Matthew, concludes. All the nations of the world are pictured as standing before the throne of the great Judge, who proceeds to divide them into two distinct classes, even as a shepherd divides the sheep from the goats. And the dividing line is drawn not between those who have committed certain sinful acts to which a definite name could be given, and those who have avoided so doing, but between those who have shown charity to their fellow men, and in that service have almost unconsciously been serving their Lord, and those who have failed so to do. No reference is made in this awe-inspiring scene to any sins of commission: sins of omission alone are mentioned. The one vital and searching question, says our Lord, which will be asked on the day when the secrets of all hearts will be disclosed, and the entire medley of human actions, words and motives comes to be assessed at a proper value, will be 'Did you in the course of your earthly pilgrimage show love to the least of My brethren; or were you so self-centred, so wrapped up in your own concerns and in the pursuit of your own ambitions, so blind of the needs of others, that you never noticed the opportunities of doing good that were presented to you?' It will be no use, He implies, pleading as excuses for failure to love a narrow sphere of work, or cramping circumstances, for there are always in our midst Christ's brethren and 'inasmuch as ye did it not to one of the least of these, ye did it not to me' (Mt. xxv. 45).

All who profess and call themselves Christians should be constantly examining themselves, not merely with reference to the positive wrong they may have done, but also to their failure to express thier discipleship in terms of service to their fellow men; for it is probably true to say that we more often leave undone the things we ought to have done than do the things we ought not to have done. And *to him that knoweth to do good, and doeth it not, to him it is sin.*

CHAPTER V

a. Retribution for the rich (v. 1–6)

1. It is clear from i. 10 that there were *rich men* known to the writer who professed the Christian faith, and that some of them may have been oppressing their less well-to-do brethren. In this section, James would appear to be writing much more generally. He is in effect holding up as a warning to all Christians, who may be tempted to worldliness, the divine judgment that awaits those who, in one way or another, misuse the gift of wealth. Neither here nor elsewhere in the New Testament are the rich denounced merely for being rich, but rather for yielding so readily to the temptations to which the rich are especially prone. The almost invariable accompaniments of great wealth are a false sense of security and an insatiable love of power; and 'all power corrupts and absolute power corrupts absolutely'. Our Lord in His teaching on this subject emphasized the self-satisfaction that so often results from the accumulation of wealth and said, 'Woe unto you that are rich! for ye have received your consolation' (Lk. vi. 24); and He told His disciples that it was very difficult for those who had great riches to enter the kingdom of God. He did not say it was impossible, for that would have been to limit the divine power (see Mk. x. 23–27). James, on the other hand, stresses the certainty of the retribution that awaits those whose wealth has led them into sin.

As at iv. 13, the author arrests the reader's attention with the words *Go to now.* He then proceeds to call upon the *rich men* to shed tears, tears not of repentance but of anguish. Assuming their unrepentance he announces, in the spirit of the Old Testament prophets, the inevitable doom that confronts them. And the inference he would wish his Christian readers to draw from this denunciation is the folly of setting a high value upon wealth, or of envying those who possess it, or of striving feverishly to obtain it. For the truth is that all who are rich without having 'poverty of spirit' are faced, whether they are aware of it or not, with swift and sure retribution at the hands of God. Because the rich are nearly always self-deceived, by thinking that their present prosperity will be permanent, James warns them that *miseries* are coming upon them. And because they imagine that by means of their wealth they can mitigate, if not render themselves immune from the sorrows and hardships that are the lot of others, James bids them *weep and howl* at the severity of the divine retribution which will fall upon them. This judgment has not already arrived; but it is so certain and so predetermined that James, in true prophetic manner, speaks of it almost as if it were a present reality, for the literal meaning of the original is that these miseries are now in the process of coming upon them.

2. The Greek verbs translated *are corrupted* and *are motheaten* are in the perfect tense. Some commentators regard this as a prophetic perfect, and assume a reference to the fate which will sooner or later overtake all material possessions. It is more natural, however, to assume that what is here being described has actually taken place. In enumerating in these verses the evils that are associated with great wealth, James draws attention first, as an observed fact, to the insatiable greed which leads to hoarding. Some rich men in their eagerness to get more and more goods have blinded themselves to the obvious fact that such goods, if not used, do and must deteriorate. It is clear from the meaning of the verb in the expression translated *Your riches are corrupted*, *sesēpen*, that the reference here is to such perishable products as corn and oil which in due course will rot if left unused. *Garments*, or 'changes of raiment', were one of the chief forms of wealth in the ancient world, being used as a means of payment, or given as presents, or handed down as heirlooms. This form of wealth is often mentioned in the Bible side by side with silver and gold, as in Paul's farewell speech to the Ephesian elders where he asserts 'I have coveted no man's silver, or gold, or apparel' (Acts xx.

33). The rich hoarders, whom James has in mind, would rather that their surplus garments should be eaten up by what the Psalmist called the 'fretting' moth (Ps. xxxix. 12, P.B.V.), than that they should become the possession of another.

3. Similarly these acquisitive misers have allowed their *gold and silver* to become *cankered.* As the latter word is somewhat archaic in this sense, the translation of the R.V. 'rusted' is preferable, particularly as it reproduces exactly the original, where a cognate verb and noun are used side by side, *katiōtai* and *ios.* To allow valuable things to perish by this neglect constitutes a great sin. For, as Calvin comments, 'God has not appointed gold for rust nor garments for moth; but on the contrary he has designed them as aids to human life'. Therefore *the rust of them*, James warns the rich whom he is apostrophizing, *shall be a witness against you*, adding fuel as it were to the fire of divine judgment. The significance of the expression *shall eat your flesh as it were fire* is that the rust which has corroded the possessions will also bring about the downfall of the possessors. As Ropes explains, 'The idea is of rust corroding and so consuming human flesh, like the wearing into the flesh of a rusty iron chain—a terrible image for the disastrous results of treating money as the chief reliance and aim of life'.

There would seem to be no doubt that the words *as it were fire* should be connected with the previous clause as in the English versions. Grammatically, however, they could be connected with what follows. In that case 'as' would have to mean 'since', and the translation, preferred by Ropes to any other, would be 'since you have stored up fire (i.e. the fire of Gehenna) which you will experience in the last days'. But this does not seem the most natural way of grouping the words; and its adoption robs the last clause of the verse of its irony. *Ye have heaped treasure together*, spending much time and exerting much effort in the process, not so much *for the last days*, as 'in the last days' (R.V.). The *last days*, though the rich are unaware of it, are in a sense already present; for this expression is used sometimes of the interval that precedes the return of the Lord in judgment as well as of the day of judgment itself. Christians are always living in the last days. Peter, for example, regarded the events of the day of Pentecost as a fulfilment now 'in the last days' of a prophecy of Joel (see Acts ii. 17). The translation *for the last days* seems to have been due to the supposition that James is here uttering the same truth as that expressed by Paul in Rom. ii. 5, 'after thy hardness and impenitent heart (thou) treasurest up unto thyself wrath against the day of wrath'. In this exegesis the treasury of accumulated wealth becomes in effect a treasury of divine wrath from which God will draw on the day of judgment. Since in several manuscripts of the Latin Vulgate 'anger' is inserted as the object of the verb in this last sentence of verse 3, it would appear that this interpretation exercised an early influence upon the text.

4. But avarice takes more than one form. It is always cruel, but on some occasions it acts with special cruelty. And in this verse James draws attention to what is perhaps the most inhuman of all its manifestations—the withholding from the labourer of the payment that is his due. In the Mosaic law the divine prohibition of this offence is clear and specific. 'Thou shalt not oppress an hired servant that is poor and needy . . . At his day thou shalt give him his hire, neither shall the sun go down upon it; for he is poor, and setteth his heart upon it: lest he cry against thee unto the Lord, and it be sin unto thee' (Dt. xxiv. 14, 15). Moreover, the *labourers*, specified by James, whose *hire is of you kept back by fraud*, are none other than the men *who have reaped down your fields*: and, as Calvin comments, 'What can be more base than that they, who supply us with bread by their labour, should be pined through want? And yet this monstrous thing is common; for there are many of such a tyrannical disposition that they think that the rest of mankind live only for their benefit.'

The certainty of the divine punishment that must be meted out upon this outstanding exhibition of man's inhumanity to man is nowhere more clearly stated than in Mal. iii. 5, where God says through the mouth of His prophet 'I will come near to you to judgment; and I will be a swift witness against . . . those that oppress the hireling in his wages'. Nor does such a sin ever escape God's notice, for *the hire* itself, says James, *crieth* for vengeance. Just as Abel's blood is said to cry unto God from the ground where it was shed (see Gn. iv. 10), and just as the cities of Sodom and Gomorrah are described as crying out because of the grievous sins that had been perpetrated within them (see Gn. xviii. 20, 21), so the money that remains in the coffers of the grasping rich, instead of being distributed in wages for service duly rendered, is here pictured as crying out to God in condemnation of its owners. Such a cry is accompanied by the cries of the afflicted themselves, and all such cries *are entered into the ears of the Lord of sabaoth*. In other words, they are most assuredly heard, and acted upon by Him. The Psalmist uses the same language about the divine answer to prayer when he says 'In my distress I called upon the Lord . . . he heard my voice out of his temple, and my cry came before him, even into his ears' (Ps. xviii. 6).

The word *sabaoth* is used in the Old Testament, so it is usually supposed by scholars, to express the truth that Jehovah is the God of the 'hosts', i.e. of the armies of Israel—both the human armies that were fighting against the heathen and the armies of heaven that came to the assistance of the people of God in their struggle against the mighty, when humanly speaking the odds were against them (see Jdg. v. 20 and 2 Ki. vi. 17). This expression 'God of sabaoth' is one of the most majestic of all the titles of God in the Old Testament, drawing attention, as it does, to His sovereign omnipotence. The Hebrew word is found transliterated, instead of being translated, only twice in the New Testament, in this passage where the language echoes Is. v. 9, and in Rom. ix. 29 where it occurs in a direct quotation from Is. i. 9. This phenomenon is explained by the fact that, in both these Old Testament passages, the Greek Septuagint version, used both by James and Paul, retains the word in its Hebrew form, instead of following its normal practice of translating it by the Greek word for 'almighty'. The use of the expression here in James emphasizes the truth that, though the poor and the oppressed appear to have no champions on earth, they have as their helper and avenger none other than the Lord God omnipotent.

5. Attention is here drawn to a third vicious trait that often characterizes the rich—luxury and extravagance. Jesus also underlined this, when He described the rich man in His parable who 'was clothed in purple and fine linen, and fared sumptuously every day' (Lk. xvi. 19). The word translated *Ye have lived in pleasure* (R.V. 'delicately'), *etruphēsate*, is probably meant to suggest an enervating life of luxury, effeminacy and self-indulgence. The cognate noun is found in Lk. vii. 25 where it describes the 'delicate' (A.V. and R.V.) living associated with kings' courts. Such luxury is sternly denounced in the Bible, and nowhere with greater emphasis and eloquence than in the book of Amos. 'Woe to them that are at ease in Zion . . . that lie upon beds of ivory, and stretch themselves upon their couches, and eat the lamb out of the flock, and the calves out of the midst of the stall . . . that drink wine in bowls, and anoint themselves with the chief ointments' (see Am. vi. 1–6).

The word *espatalēsate*, translated in the A.V. *and been wanton*, and in the R.V. 'and taken your pleasure', probably suggests extravagance and waste,[1] though Hort, after a careful study of the word, concluded that the two verbs in this clause have much the same meaning. It is, however, unlikely that James would use two comparatively rare words in juxtaposition if no further idea had been conveyed by the second. Ropes was of the opinion that it suggests 'positive lewdness and riotousness. The R.V. "taken your pleasure" is weaker than the original and not so good as the antiquated "been wanton" of the A.V.' In the only other place in the New Testament where the word occurs, 1 Tim. v. 6, it describes the widow with extravagant ideas who 'is dead while she liveth' and is not 'a widow indeed'. The waste that results from extravagance is as abhorrent to God as the waste that is due to hoarding and neglect.

In the expression *as in a day of slaughter* the A.V. follows the reading found in the later manuscripts. The R.V., following more ancient authorities, omits 'as'. Earlier commentators using the text of Erasmus concluded that the words 'as in a day of slaughter' were added by James to give a fuller des-

[1] *Synonyms of the New Testament*, R. C. Trench, p. 193.

cription of the extravagant living in which the luxurious indulge. Thus Tyndale's marginal note to his translation at this point reads, 'i.e. when men kill beasts to make cheer and as the Jews did in their thankofferings and freewill offerings'. It is, however, probable that the word 'as' should be omitted, and that the expression *in a day of slaughter* is contrasted with *on the earth* and should be interpreted as a reference to the day of judgment. God's judgments in history are sometimes described in the Old Testament as times of 'slaughter' (see Is. xxxiv. 6; Ezk. xxi. 15). Just as beasts continue to fatten themselves, unconscious that they are really being made ready for slaughter, so the sinful rich are pictured as *nourishing their hearts*, filling their lives with every conceivable form of pleasure, while still *on the earth*, so as to be 'ready', though they are wholly unaware of it, for 'the day of slaughter', when the doom that inevitably awaits them will descend upon them, as the Lord comes in judgment.

6. The last evil to which James alludes as the climax of his present denunciation of the rich, is their oppression, even unto death, of the righteous, to whom their ways are abhorrent, and who are too weak to resist them. The language in which this shameful persecution is here described, would seem to be reminiscent of the following passage in the book Wisdom, where the reasoning of the ungodly about the righteous man, culminating in their decision to put him to death in order to test the reality of his faith in God and his powers of endurance under suffering, are so graphically described.

> 'Let us see if his words be true,
> And let us try what shall befall in the ending of his life.
> For if the righteous man is God's son, he will uphold him,
> And he will deliver him out of the hand of his adversaries.
> With outrage and torture let us put him to the test,
> That we may learn his gentleness, and may prove his patience under wrong.
> Let us condemn him to a shameful death;
> For he shall be visited according to his words.'
>
> (Wisdom ii. 17–20, R.V.)

In the light of this passage from Wisdom it is almost certain that *the just* (R.V. the righteous one) should be regarded as a general description of the saints of God, as in 1 Pet. iv. 18, and that the reference should not be limited to Jesus in spite of the fact that He is designated 'the Just One' three times in Acts (iii. 14, vii. 52, xxii. 14). If James had intended a direct reference to Him at this point, we may be sure that it would have been more specific.

If the last clause is read as a question instead of a statement, as Hort suggested and as Ropes advocates, the sense is entirely changed. Assuming the subject of the verb to be *the just* the meaning would be that, although now he is too impotent to offer practical resistance, he wills to resist, and his resistance will become effective on the day of judgment when he will testify against his oppressors. The question 'Does not the righteous man resist you?' would thus have a prophetic character, and the answer expected would be the affirmative. The same considerations would apply if 'the Lord' is regarded as the subject of the verb. God's determination to offer resistance, though not immediately obvious, will be effective on the day of judgment. The rendering in A.V. would seem, however, to be much more probable; it is in keeping with our Lord's words in the sermon on the mount (Mt. v. 39) and with Paul's injunction in Rom. xii. 19, and it brings the section to an end on a note of majestic pathos. *He doth not resist you.*

b. Patience in view of the coming of the Lord (v. 7–11)

7. After declaring the certain judgment that awaits the rich for their miserliness, their exploitation of the weak, their luxury and their extravagance James proceeds to exhort his Christian readers not to lose patience if the day should seem to be long delayed when 'the mighty shall be put down from their seats and the rich sent empty away'—the day when the oppressed shall be delivered from all the wrongs they have unjustly suffered and their oppressors sentenced to the punishment they deserve. The temptation to lose patience may lead all who yield to it to the sins to which impatience so easily gives rise —vindictiveness and despair. There is, accordingly, significance in each word of the writer's earnest and tender appea *Be patient therefore, brethren.*

The verb used here for *Be patient*, *makrothumēsate*, together with its cognate noun, usually rendered 'long-suffering', denotes not so much the brave endurance of afflictions and the refusal to give way before them even under pressure, as the self-restraint which enables the sufferer to refrain from hasty retaliation. The opposites of 'patience' in this sense are wrath and revenge. When the Bible speaks of the patience of God with humanity, as in Rom. ii. 4 and 1 Pet. iii. 20, it is significantly these words that are used. God is patient because He is 'slow to anger' and 'of great kindness', and does not speedily inflict upon transgressors the full punishment they deserve. Nor does He, in executing judgment and assessing penalties, apply the letter of the law with all the strictness and exactness of an over-scrupulous judge. He recognizes, as the best human judges recognize, that sometimes circumstances alter cases; and He gives the offender plenty of time to repent. He is, in a word, long-suffering towards them, though there comes a time when His patience is exhausted; and the final day of His wrath must dawn upon the unrepentant sinner. If the all-holy God, faced with the enormity of human sin, is patient, so too, James implies, should the Christian be patient in the face of the injustices of human life. His patience must be extended both towards God and his fellow men. He must not be impatient with God for failing to avenge His faithful people immediately; nor must he attempt to vindicate himself by assuming the role of judge of his fellow men. And the power to exercise this patience is available for him just so far as he submits himself to the Holy Spirit, for a fruit of that Spirit is long-suffering (Gal. v. 22).

The particular word used for *coming* in this verse, *parousia*, is used also by Peter, Paul, and John, and by Jesus Himself with reference to His appearing in glory. It was current among the Greeks to describe the official visits of a monarch to a city within his dominions. On such state occasions the royal 'presence' (for that is the literal meaning of the word) was such that none could fail to recognize the Sovereign for what in fact he was. By the use of this word in the New Testament for the second coming of Christ, that second coming is contrasted with His first. As the babe of Bethlehem, the carpenter of Nazareth, the Son of Man with nowhere to lay His head, despised and rejected of men, Christ came, so to speak, *incognito*. It was only veiled in flesh that His Godhead could be seen during His earthly life, and then only with the eyes of faith. But His appearance on the clouds of heaven will be such that He will be conspicuous, without any possibility of doubt, as the Judge of mankind, as the Lord from heaven, who will gather His elect together, and summon those already living in union with Him to be with Him for ever and share with Him His eternal glory. The Christian is now living between these two comings of his Lord, and he looks both backward to the first and forward to the second for inspiration during his earthly pilgrimage. Consequently patience for him is not what it is wont to be for those who have no share in the Christian hope—a dumb, helpless, passive virtue, 'close-lipped' and 'sad . . . too near neighbour to despair'. On the contrary, he runs with patience the race set before him, looking unto Jesus the author and finisher of his faith who endured the cross despising the shame (see Heb. xii. 1, 2). And when he is tempted to break out into uncontrolled wrath in face of unjust persecution, he looks forward to the parousia of his Lord and sees how futile, how unworthy, and how ineffective are his own attempts at vindicating his rights in view of the certain return of Him who alone has power to execute true and righteous judgment. By such patience he is able to gain possession of his soul (see Lk. xxi. 19).

As an illustration of the patience which is active and creative just because it is directed towards a specific end, the patience which is the child of faith and hope, James cites the *husbandman* waiting for the *precious fruit of the earth*. Such fruit is 'precious' because on its production the maintenance of physical life depends, just as in 1 Pet. i. 19 the blood of Christ is described as 'precious' because by the shedding of it, and by nothing else, redemption and the life of holiness have become possible. There is nothing in the original to justify the insertion of the word *long* before patience, and it is omitted in R.V. and R.S.V. As a matter of fact, the time between seedtime, or the first appearance of the blade, and harvest was roughly speaking four months (see Jn. iv. 35); not a very long period, but fraught with much anxiety in a country which was utterly dependent upon *the early and latter rain*, the first due soon after sowing and the second when the crop was ripening. The faithful Jew knew, however, that God would be true to His promise that if His people kept His commandments, He would give them 'the first rain and the latter rain' (Dt. xi. 14); and the prophet bids the children of Zion be glad and rejoice in the Lord because He caused to come down for them 'the former and the latter rain' (Joel ii. 23). So the farmer's patience *for* (R.V. 'over') his land was more in the nature of confident expectancy. His faith in the reliability of God acted as a restraining and controlling influence during what might otherwise have been a time of acute and enervating anxiety. In the same way, the faithful Christian knows that Christ will be true to His promise to come again to His people; and, even though the period of time that is destined to elapse before that return takes place cannot be estimated in the same way that the farmer may reasonably determine the date of harvest, nevertheless the Christian's patience is firmly grounded upon the certainty of his faith.

8. Nothing strikes such fearfulness into the human heart as anxiety due to uncertainty about ultimate issues. For example, if we knew beyond doubt that a serious illness would result in a complete recovery of health, even though the length of time that must pass before that happy event remained unknown to us, much of the burden of our anxiety would be shed. Similarly, though at a much higher and more important level, the Christian is not meant to be worried about the number of years that may pass before the *parousia* of the Lord. He is called upon to *stablish* (i.e. 'strengthen') his heart in the assurance that his Lord's return will bring to him complete spiritual health, full salvation and eternal life. Moreover, for him, the thought of eternity so dominates and controls the thought of time, that in his reckoning, time always seems to be a *short* time (see 1 Cor. vii. 29). In other words, he lives so constantly under the influence of the *parousia* that it can truly be said that for him *the Lord draweth nigh.* The literal translation of these last words is 'has drawn nigh'. The same expression is used in 1 Pet. iv. 7 of 'the end of all things', and in Mk. i. 15 of 'the kingdom of God'. R.V. and R.S.V. translate in this verse of James 'the coming of the Lord is at hand'.

If the Lord's return seems to us to be long delayed, or if we relegate it to such a remote future that it has no effect upon our outlook or way of living, it is clear that it has ceased to be for us a *living* hope; and it may be that we have allowed the doctrine that 'He will come again with glory to judge both the quick and the dead' to be whittled away by scepticism, or to be so transmuted into something else, such as the gradual transformation of human society by Christian values, that it has ceased to exercise any powerful influence on our lives.

9. During the period of waiting for the Lord's return, particularly in days of persecution and severe trial, Christians are tempted to blame one another for the miseries of their present situation. It is this temptation which James seems to have in mind when he says *Grudge not one against another, brethren.* The word *grudge* is archaic in the sense of 'complain' which is what the Greek word *stenazete* implies. A.V. margin renders 'groan', R.V. 'murmur' and R.S.V. 'grumble'. Christians may indeed groan under their individual sufferings, for they are not supermen impervious to grief, but they are not to groan or complain *one against another.* All of them are equally prone to such afflictions, and no particular individuals are solely responsible for them. Mutual recrimination is therefore both useless and sinful, and brings with it the risk of condemnation—to be experienced perhaps sooner than those who indulge in it may be aware. For *the judge*, who alone has complete knowledge of every human thought, word and act, and who alone is free from all partiality, *standeth*, says James, echoing the words of Jesus, *before the door* (see Mk. xiii. 29). His foot is already upon the doorstep; and at His final coming no human being can bar

His entrance. The thought of the Lord's return is thus a warning as well as a consolation to Christians.

10. James here bids his Christian brethren remember that the affliction, which should call forth their patience and long-suffering during their earthly probation, has always been the lot of God's saints; and it has never detracted from their blessedness. He illustrates this by drawing their attention to the company of men who would most readily be accounted among the blessed, particularly by Jewish Christians. So far from such affliction plunging 'the goodly fellowship of the prophets' into misery and despair, and causing them to become faithless, it aided them as they trod their appointed way of salvation. Jesus had bidden His disciples rejoice when they were reviled and persecuted for His sake, for, He added, 'so persecuted they the prophets which were before you' (Mt. v. 11, 12). Thus did He remind them of the privilege as well as of the certainty of their suffering. Stephen in his defence put this pertinent question to his accusers 'which of the prophets have not your fathers persecuted?' (Acts vii. 52). So James bids his readers 'Take for an example of suffering affliction and of patience the prophets who have spoken in the name of the Lord' (i.e. as the Lord's representatives, speaking with His authority and power).

There is hardly a prophet about whom we have any biographical or autobiographical information in the Old Testament who could not be shown to be in some way *an example of suffering affliction, and of patience*. But of all the prophets, whom James must have had in mind, perhaps the most outstanding in this connection is Jeremiah, who later became known as '*the* prophet', so frequently did the Jews of subsequent generations look back to him for inspiration and courage in their own trials and persecutions. This hyper-sensitive, warm-hearted patriot, compelled to proclaim a succession of divine messages to his countrymen that were unpopular because they were of necessity pessimistic, who was so sympathetic towards the sufferings of others, was himself beaten, put in the stocks, imprisoned in a dungeon, and thrown into a cistern by the very men whom he would gladly have saved, if such salvation had been possible, from the doom that awaited them. His life was one of almost perpetual physical and spiritual suffering, yet his demeanour throughout was such that, of all the historical characters of the Old Testament, he is the one who most foreshadowed Him who, when He was reviled, reviled not again, and who suffered for man's salvation the physical and spiritual agony of the cross.

11. Constancy under suffering is by general consent an admirable quality. It is certainly regarded as such in the Bible. 'Blessed is he that waiteth' (i.e. endureth) we read in Dn. xii. 12. Our Lord Himself pronounced a benediction upon those who are persecuted for righteousness' sake (Mt. v. 10). Not only did He warn His disciples that they would be hated by all men for His name's sake, but He added words of great challenge and hope, 'he that endureth to the end shall be saved' (see Mt. x. 22). James aligns himself with this biblical judgment when he writes *we count them happy* (R.V., better, 'call them blessed') *which endure* (R.V., following a better reading, 'which endured', blessedness being the certain result of endurance but not necessarily always accompanying it).

It is important to notice that the word here translated *patience*, *hupomonē*, and used to describe the great virtue of Job, with whose story James assumes his readers to be familiar, is cognate with the verb translated in the previous clause *which endure*. It is not the same word as that used for patience in the other verses of this section, and expresses a determination to face a particular trial or a series of trials without flinching. 'No English word', wrote Hort, 'is quite strong enough to express the active courage and resolution here implied. "Constancy" or "endurance" comes nearest, and the latter has the advantage of preserving the parallelism of the previous verb.' R.V. retains 'patience' in the text, perhaps because 'the patience of Job' had become so proverbial, but gives 'endurance' as an alternative in the margin. R.S.V. renders 'steadfastness'. It is not so much the self-restraint of Job under affliction, leading him to be patient with others, that is here emphasized, for Job was very far from showing patience in this sense with his so-called comforters. What Job did, however, display in a marked degree was a determination to endure whatever might fall to his lot without losing faith in God. He believed even when he could not understand.

When blow after blow had fallen upon him in rapid succession Job cried, 'Naked came I out of my mother's womb, and naked shall I return thither: the Lord gave, and the Lord hath taken away; blessed be the name of the Lord' (Job i. 21). His reply to his wife when she invited him to curse God and die was, 'Thou speakest as one of the foolish women speaketh. What? shall we receive good at the hand of God, and shall we not receive evil' (Job ii. 10). To 'the physicians of no value' who posed as his friends his answer was, 'Though he slay me, yet will I trust in him' (xiii. 15). He was convinced that 'his witness was in heaven and his record with the most high' (see xvi. 19); and he knew that his Redeemer was alive (see xix. 28).

The end of the Lord was the complete vindication of Job by his Maker. Not only were his material possessions and his worldly prosperity restored to him, but he was granted a fuller understanding of the mystery of the divine purpose, and a more direct experience of the majesty and sovereignty of Almighty God; and he became capable of a greater and deeper penitence. 'I have heard of thee by the hearing of the ear', he was able to cry, 'but now mine eye seeth thee. Wherefore I abhor myself, and repent in dust and ashes' (xlii. 5, 6). So it was that 'the Lord blessed the latter end of Job more than his beginning' (xlii. 12). The God, whose severity Job had for so long experienced, as his character was tested in the furnace of affliction, in the end showed Himself to be, in the words of the Psalmist quoted by James, *very pitiful, and of tender mercy* (see Ps. ciii. 8).

c. Swearing forbidden (v. 12)

12. *Above all things* must not be interpreted absolutely but in reference to the preceding passage. For the writer does not mean to suggest that swearing is a worse offence than stealing, adultery, or murder. Nor is he just speaking in hyperbole. What he means is that of all the manifestations of impatience in times of stress and affliction the most frequent is the taking of the Lord's name in vain by the use of explosive utterances and hasty and irreverent oaths. The injunction *swear not* is not a prohibition of oaths altogether. Solemn statements made under oath in a court of law about matters of supreme moment, involving perhaps the life or death of an individual, are not here in the writer's mind. What James is denouncing is the levity with which the name of God, or some substitute for the name of God used to satisfy Pharisaic scruples, tended to be uttered when men's minds were disordered by impatience, and self-control was abandoned. The additional words *neither by the earth, neither by any other oath*, are parallel to the words used by Jesus in the sermon on the mount, when He was attacking the casuistry of the Pharisees in allowing the use of frivolous oaths, such as those taken by heaven, by earth, by Jerusalem, or by one's head, on the ground that the name of God was not actually mentioned. Such oaths, the Pharisees maintained, were of no account. Our Lord's view, however, was that it was impossible to differentiate in this subtle way between God and what belonged to God; and the very use of such subterfuge was in itself dishonouring to God. He therefore prohibited altogether the use of oaths in ordinary conversations. 'Swear not all', He said: and James here reiterates His teaching (see Mt. v. 33–36).

The way to avoid swearing of this kind is by being strictly truthful in ordinary speech, avoiding exaggeration, so often indulged in to create an impression, eschewing the half-truth which conceals the lie, and generally aiming at simplicity and straight-forwardness. Sometimes it is the fear that their words will not be taken at their face value which leads men to try and reinforce them by swearing; and that in itself is a reflection upon the insincerity and duplicity which so often characterize conversation. Men should say what they mean, and mean what they say. James' instruction therefore is *let your yea be yea; and your nay, nay*. 'Yes' should mean yes without any reservations. A variant, and almost certainly secondary, reading found in some MSS. is 'let your speech be yea, yea; nay, nay'.

This brings the passage verbally into line with Mt. v. 37. It is not, however, at all certain that our Lord in this utterance is commending emphatic speech, for His words might be translated 'let your word yea really mean yea, and your nay mean nay', which is precisely what the ordinary reading here in James is saying. The teaching of both Jesus and James on this matter is virtually the same.

The danger that confronts all who indulge in frivolous oaths is the violation of the third commandment in the divine decalogue, where it is specifically stated that 'the Lord will not hold him guiltless that taketh His name in vain'. Sincerity in speech must therefore be aimed at, says James, *lest ye fall into condemnation.* The text of Erasmus, followed by Tyndale, reads 'lest ye fall into hypocrisy'. This, as Calvin noticed, gives a sense not unsuitable to the context; for any avoidance of simplicity and directness in speech leads to dissimulation. It is, however, much the slighter reading and is not really in keeping with the severity of the passage. The reading of the A.V. follows the text of Elzevir and is based upon better manuscript evidence; and it has rightly been followed by subsequent English versions either in the form 'under judgement' (R.V.), or 'under condemnation' (R.S.V.).

There are few spheres of conduct in which the young Christian today needs to take the injunctions of the Epistle of James more to heart than in this matter of frivolous and indiscriminate oaths and the thoughtless mention of the divine name in general conversation. Not only is he guilty of violating the divine law on this subject, but his power of witnessing to others is rendered ineffective. For even those who do not recognize the existence of God are the first to notice the inconsistency and hypocrisy of those who profess to worship Him but who do not hesitate to use His name promiscuously. Moreover, the serious taking of oaths, when we are called to do so as witnesses in a court of law, must lose much of its dignity and solemnity if we are accustomed to use God's name freely and glibly. It was with good purpose that part of the instruction given to his children by the author of Ecclesiasticus, a book with which James was probably familiar, ran as follows:

'Accustom not thy mouth to an oath;
And be not accustomed to the naming of the Holy One.
For as a servant that is continually scourged shall not lack a bruise,
So he also that sweareth and nameth God continually shall not be cleansed from sin.'
(Ecclus. xxiii. 9, 10, R.V.)

d. Prayer under all circumstances (v. 13–18)

13. Instead of resorting to mutual recrimination under the trials of their earthly life, or impetuously breaking out into oaths, Christians are here bidden to turn constantly to prayer, whatever the circumstances of their life may be. The habit of prayer should be, and indeed is, one of the most obvious features which differentiates a Christian from other people. He knows that his heavenly Father extends to him a standing invitation to draw near to Himself, which no experience of joy or sorrow and no conditions of prosperity or adversity have any power to cancel. The shed blood of Jesus has opened up for him a way of direct access into the divine presence, and that way is never barred. The believer can turn immediately for inspiration, peace, and power to Him who holds the universe in the palm of His hand, and orders all things in accordance with His sovereign will, with the assurance that 'all things work together for good to them that love God, to them who are the called according to his purpose' (Rom. viii. 28), and knowing that 'the eyes of the Lord are over the righteous, and his ears are open unto their prayers' (1 Pet. iii. 12). The natural man, who knows not God, is without this privilege; and the result is that he tends to be unduly elated in times of success and prosperity, and to be plunged into depression and despair when he is the victim of untoward circumstances or vexed with pain and sorrow. It is very difficult for him 'to meet with triumph and disaster and treat these two impostors just the same', though this may be his Stoic ideal. The Christian, on the other hand, because of the steadying influence of prayer, can say with the apostle Paul, 'I know both how to be abased, and I know how to abound: every where and in all things I am instructed both to be full and to be hungry, both to abound and to suffer need. I can do all things through Christ which strengtheneth me' (Phil. iv. 12, 13).

Is any among you afflicted? James asks in a vivid rhetorical question, which is in effect the protasis of a conditional sentence 'If any is afflicted'. The verb he here uses, *kakopathei*, is cognate with the noun which summarized in verse 10 the numerous troubles and calamities that befell the Old Testament prophets when they spoke in the name of the Lord. The same word is used in the second Epistle to Timothy to describe the afflictions which the Christian evangelist may be called to endure (see 2 Tim. ii. 9, iv. 5). In such circumstances, let not the Christian, James implies, indulge in any introspective self-pity, but *let him pray*. It was, we remember, when Jesus was in *agony*, wrestling with the forces of evil at the moment of their strongest attack, that 'he prayed more earnestly' (Lk. xxii. 44). Prayer may not remove the affliction but it most certainly can transform it.

But, though the Christian can often find joy even in affliction through the assurance, which comes to him in prayer, that it is in accordance with the purposes of God, his life is far from being one of continual adversity. It has its times of merriment as well. The verb used by James in the interrogation *Is any merry?* (R.V. 'cheerful'), *euthumei*, is found with its cognates only here and in Acts in the Greek Bible. In Acts it is used by Paul on two notable occasions, both times of outward trial and difficulty. He makes his defence 'the more cheerfully' before the Roman procurator Felix, for 'I know', he says, 'that thou hast been of many years a judge unto this nation' (Acts xxiv. 10). And during the perilous voyage to Rome, after a long period of abstinence from food, Paul bids his shipmates 'be of good cheer', the ground for such an exhortation being the assurance that has come to him through supernatural means that all the occupants of the vessel will reach land in safety (Acts xxvii. 25). Cheerfulness in adversity can indeed be displayed by Christians. James is thinking here, however, more of the cheerfulness that is unconnected with adversity. A good thing in itself, such cheerfulness becomes a bad thing if it tends to draw the Christian away from God. Accordingly, without in any way bidding him abandon it, James reminds him of one great outlet for exuberant spirits, which will banish any danger of profanity. *Let him sing psalms* (R.V. 'let him sing praise').

The Greek verb here used, *psallō*, from which the English word 'psalm' is derived, originally meant to play by touching a stringed instrument, and then to sing to the accompaniment of the harp. It is used in Rom. xv. 9, in a quotation from Ps. xviii, of the general celebration of God's praises. 'I will sing unto thy name.' In Eph. v. 19 it refers to the music of the heart, 'singing and making melody in your heart to the Lord'. And in 1 Cor. xiv. 15 it describes the stirring of the soul which must be present in all genuine worship. 'I will sing with the spirit.' The word cannot then, in the present context, be restricted to the singing of the psalms of David. It must be given a wider reference to every sounding of God's praises, whether in the company of others or alone, whether vocally with or without musical accompaniment, or silently.

14. The reference in this verse to *anointing with oil* has received disproportionate attention in the Church owing to the erroneous justification which Roman Catholics have found in it for the so-called sacrament of extreme unction. In that ceremony the priest anoints the eyes, ears, nostrils, hands and feet of a sick person considered to be *in extremis* in the belief that the application of such previously consecrated oil is an effective medium of forgiveness in the case of those who are no longer able to make conscious confession of sins and receive priestly absolution. In the Douay version of the Bible, the official Roman Catholic English translation, we find the following footnote to this verse. 'See here a plain warrant of scripture for the Sacrament of Extreme Unction, that any controversy against its institution would be against the express words of the sacred text in the plainest terms.' A further mishandling of this text is to be found in the translation in that version of the word *elders* by 'priests', in spite of the fact that the Latin Vulgate, from which the version was made, has *presbuteros* and not *sacerdotes*, the usual word for priests. It is significant that the Greek word for priest, *hiereus*, is never found in the New Testament with reference to the Christian ministry, but, apart from the Jewish priesthood, is reserved for Christ alone. It is to the credit of R. A. Knox that, in his recent translation of the Vulgate, he uses 'presbyters' in this passage.

That this verse will not bear such an interpretation as Catholicism has placed upon it becomes clear when it is carefully examined. The main subject of the section in which it occurs is Christian prayer, by which divine help and blessing are conveyed to the Christian in response either to his own prayers or the intercession of other Christians on his behalf. In *all* circumstances, the writer insists, such prayer is the Christian's duty and privilege, in sickness as well as in health. In the case of serious illness, however, when the body may be racked with pain and the mind considerably disturbed, it is not easy for the sufferer unaided to turn his thoughts in any articulate or concentrated manner to prayer, and he needs the consolation of other Christians in what may be for him a period of much spiritual distress. James, accordingly, bids any of his readers who may find himself in such a condition *call for the elders of the church*, men it may be assumed specially blessed by the grace of the Holy Spirit, and, he adds, *let them pray over him.* While it is true that they could intercede for the sick man without being present at his bedside, nevertheless, by coming to the actual scene of suffering and by praying within sight and hearing of the sufferer himself, not only is their prayer likely to be more heart-felt and fervid, but the stricken man may well become more conscious of the effective power of prayer uttered in faith, by which, even in moments of the most acute physical weakness, communion with God can be maintained.

The object of the elders' prayer, however, is not primarily to prepare the sick man for death; and indeed nothing is said about the likelihood of his immediate decease. On the contrary, it is implied in the following verse that, if God should be graciously pleased to answer their petitions, the restoration of the sufferer to health may be rendered possible. As an accompaniment to prayer for his recovery James bids the elders *anoint him with oil in the name of the Lord.* No mention is made of any previous 'consecration' of the oil; and it might not unnaturally be supposed that the reference here is to the curative power of oil, such as is mentioned metaphorically in Is. i. 6, where the prophet complains that 'the wounds, and bruises, and festering sores . . . have not been closed, neither bound up, neither mollified with oil' (R.V.), and literally in our Lord's parable where the good Samaritan pours oil and wine into the wounds of the man lying half-dead by the roadside (Lk. x. 34). But, while oil was undoubtedly believed to possess medicinal properties in connection with certain maladies, it would not have been regarded as beneficial in all circumstances; and it is a general injunction for times of sickness that James is here giving.

It is therefore more probable that the mention of oil in this passage is to be regarded as one of the accompaniments of that *miraculous* healing which was no infrequent occurrence in the apostolic age, and is regarded in the New Testament as a supernatural sign vindicating the truth of the Christian gospel in the early days of its proclamation. It is not here assumed that in every case of sickness such miraculous healing will result from *anointing with oil in the name of the Lord*, for the result anticipated in verse 15 is contingent upon the prayer of faith being answered. Neither is it implied that oil is the necessary accompaniment of such cures, nor indeed that any material medium at all must be used. It is true that the apostles, when they were sent forth on their Galilean mission during their Lord's earthly life, endowed with His healing power 'anointed with oil many that were sick, and healed them' (Mk. vi. 13); but in the instructions given by the Lord to His apostles after His resurrection, when He despatched them on a world-wide mission, it is stated that among the 'signs following' would be the recovery of the sick after the laying-on of the apostles' hands, and there is no mention of anointing with oil (Mk. xvi. 18). It was the Holy Spirit who, after the name of the Lord Jusus had been invoked, effected these miraculous cures in the apostolic age, not the oil, nor the laying-on of hands which are often mentioned in connection with them; just as it was the power that went forth from the Lord Himself that resulted in the cure of many diseases and afflictions during His earthly ministry, and not the material elements which He sometimes used such as the clay made with saliva with which He anointed the blind man's eyes. The purpose of the use by the elders of oil in the name of the Lord, as they prayed over the sick man, was we may assume the same as the use by the apostles of the laying-on of hands. It helped in certain cases by the application of a substance that could be felt by the patient to reinforce the evidence of the ear that the Lord was being invoked by the prayer of faith to bestow upon him, if it should be His will, a miraculous cure. Moreover, the emphasis on *in the name of the Lord* made it clear that, if a cure was effected, it was the Lord's doing and not man's. Peter, we remember, was very insistent that it was not through the apostles' own power or holiness that the lame man at the gate of the temple had been made to walk (see Acts iii. 12).

If this line of interpretation is right, it follows that this verse cannot be appealed to as evidence that the Lord has committed to His Church *for all time* the power of miraculous healing. Nor can we deduce from it that anointing of the sick with oil consecrated by priests should for Christians either supplement as a matter of course the work of medical practitioners in the healing of disease, or be regarded as a means of sacramental benediction when hope of a cure through ordinary channels has been abandoned. As Calvin truly said, 'The Lord, doubtless, is present with His people in all ages, and cures their sicknesses as often as there is need, not less than formerly; and yet He does not exert these manifest powers, nor dispense miracles by the hands of apostles, because that gift was temporary'.[1] Unction is therefore not to be regarded as a sacrament, for it was not ordained by Christ Himself to be a permanent institution in His Church. It has grown up, as the twenty-fifth Article of Religion in the Book of Common Prayer implies, through a corrupt following of the apostles when the Christian ministry claimed apostolic powers. The only unction

[1] *Institutes of the Christian Religion*, Book IV, xix. 19.

of which the New Testament speaks as a permanent possession of the Christian in every age, by which he is continually invigorated and enlightened, is the unction of the Holy Spirit. 'The anointing which ye have received of him', says John, 'abideth in you' (1 Jn. ii. 27).

15. The description of the elders' prayer in this verse as *the prayer of faith* does not differentiate it in any way from other kinds of prayer, for there can be no Christian prayer at all without faith; nor does it imply that, if only there is a sufficient degree of faith, prayer will be answered. Rather would it appear to draw attention to the great truth, so much emphasized in this section, that in no circumstances of life is faith impossible; and therefore there is no situation in which Christians cannot resort to prayer. The dying thief at Calvary was capable both of faith and the prayer of faith, when nothing else was possible for him; and his prayer was effective. Similarly, the prayer of the elders on behalf of the sick man, expressing as it did his belief and their belief in the sovereignty of Almighty God, was prayer such as God would not fail to listen to. All prayer, however, is subject to the reservation 'Thy will be done'; but, provided that this limiting condition is always in the mind of him who prays, Jesus has promised 'All things, whatsoever ye shall ask in prayer, believing, ye shall receive' (Mt. xxi. 22). Much current teaching in the contemporary church on the subject of 'spiritual healing' rests on the false assumption that it is God's will that everybody should enjoy at all times perfect physical health. There is nothing in the New Testament to justify this assumption, and some evidence which points in the opposite direction. For example, Paul's 'thorn in the flesh' was not removed by God though he prayed three times that it might be taken from him.

The expression *shall save*, in this context, must mean 'shall restore to physical health'; for the New Testament nowhere asserts that men are saved, in a spiritual sense, by prayer; and it is illegitimate to limit the meaning, as some Roman Catholic commentators have tried to do, to spiritual comfort so that the passage may be made more obviously applicable to prayer accompanying extreme unction.

The Greek word here used for *the sick*, *ton kamnonta*, is found nowhere else in the New Testament. It is the present participle of a verb whose primary meaning is 'to grow weary', with the secondary sense of growing weary by reason of sickness. In its past tenses it was sometimes used as a description of 'the dead'; but as there is no instance of the present participle conveying the meaning of 'the dying', it is most improbable that that is the sense here, and that the writer means to suggest that the sufferer is *in extremis*. Similarly, the expression *shall raise him up* cannot be interpreted in a spiritual sense, but must mean 'shall enable him to stand on his feet'. The verb *egerei*, used here in a transitive sense with *the Lord* as the subject, is used intransitively at the beginning of the command given by Jesus to the paralytic 'Arise, take up thy bed, and walk' (Mk. ii. 9).

There is no suggestion in the conditional clause, *and if he have committed sins*, that the man in question may not have sinned at all; nor is the thought that the prayer of the elders will *ipso facto* secure forgiveness to be found in the words *they shall be forgiven him*. The meaning seems to be that, if God should effect a miraculous cure in answer to the elders' prayer of faith accompanied by anointing with oil in the name of the Lord, that would be a clear indication that any sins of the sufferer, which might have been responsible for this particular illness, were forgiven. It was the sight of the paralytic taking up his mattress and walking that provided unmistakable evidence that his sins, which had clearly resulted in his affliction, really had been forgiven. The New Testament does not teach that all physical suffering is due to the sins of the sufferer concerned, but that sometimes this is so is recognized by both Jesus and Paul (see Mk. ii. 5–11; 1 Cor. xi. 30).

16. The R.V., following the most ancient MSS., adds the word 'therefore' after *confess* and substitutes 'sins' for *faults*. The alterations found in the later MSS. and followed by Erasmus and the A.V. may well have been intentional, made in the interests of sound exegesis, first to prevent readers from assuming that there is a very close connection between this verse and what has preceded it, and, secondly, to make it clear that James is not necessarily here advocating a general confession by Christians to one another of *all* their sins. Even if 'therefore' is part of the original text, there is no need to insist upon a close connection with verse 15 by assuming that the text implies that the sick man and the elders have made mutual confession of sins, or that a preliminary obligation has been laid upon him to confess his trespasses to those whom he may have wronged before he could expect to be healed; though such a demand would have been in keeping with the Lord's injunction in Mt. v. 23. The connecting link between all the verses in this section would appear to be the power of prayer. In verse 16 James seems to be insisting that, if *the prayer of faith* can have such a miraculous result as that mentioned in the previous verse, Christians should always pray for one another, not only in time of illness but in all the vicissitudes of their lives, so that healing, in the fullest and widest sense of that word, may be bestowed upon them. And in order that their prayers may be intelligent and based on specific knowledge, they should not hesitate to confess to one another their *faults*, so that their brethren may bring these faults to the throne of grace.

It is clear that the makers of the A.V. regarded the Greek word *paraptōma*, which they are here translating, as having in some contexts in the New Testament a less serious implication than the word *hamartia*, the other reading in this passage usually translated 'sin'. Their rendering here and in Gal. vi. 1 of *paraptōmata* by 'faults' is sufficient evidence of this. Instances are given by Moulton and Milligan[1] of the word having the meaning in the papyri of 'slips', or 'lapses', rather than of wilful sins; though they rightly add that 'they do not purpose to define the word in the New Testament occurrences from these instances'. It is true that in very many passages it is very difficult to draw any marked distinction between the force of these two words, but R. C. Trench is probably justified in saying that 'sometimes *paraptōma* is used when it is intended to

[1] *The Vocabulary of the Greek Testament.*

designate sins not of the deepest dye and the worst enormity'.[1] In any case, it would seem that it is not a legitimate inference from this passage to suppose that James is exhorting his readers either to make a public confession of *all* their sins without restraint to their fellow Christians in a general assembly, or to unbosom themselves *completely* even to chosen individuals in private. The former practice, indulged in somewhat freely in recent years by members of 'the Moral-Rearmament Movement', is apt to have more harmful than beneficial results. Only too often it gives an outlet for an unhealthy exhibitionism; nor is it always prompted by the desire to elicit the prayers of others on behalf of the sinner, which James seems to suggest is the main purpose of the mutual confession he is here advocating. There would seem to be little doubt that the *faults* he has chiefly in mind are offences against other brethren, which spoil their fellowship one with another and make it difficult, if not impossible, for them to worship together as the people of God. It was of these offences that Jesus explicitly stated 'If thou bring thy gift to the altar, and there rememberest that thy brother hath ought against thee; leave there thy gift before the altar, and go thy way; first be reconciled to thy brother, and then come and offer thy gift' (Mt. v. 23, 24). Beyond this, it would seem that Christians must use their discretion as to the extent to which, and the people to whom they are prepared to divulge their sins of thought, word and deed. Calvin spoke wisely on this subject when he wrote:[2] 'Confession of this nature ought to be free so as not to be exacted of all, but only recommended to those who feel they have need of it; and, even those who use it according to their necessity must neither be compelled by any precept, nor artfully induced to enumerate all their sins, but only insofar as they shall deem it for their interest, that they may obtain the full benefit of consolation.'

It need scarcely be added that the use of this verse by Roman Catholic exegetes as a justification for the practice of auricular confession to a priest is entirely unjustified. Martin

[1] *Synonyms of the New Testament*, p. 235.
[2] *Institutes of the Christian Religion*, Book III, chapter iv.

Luther said in connection with such an interpretation: 'A strange confessor! His name is "One another".' Nevertheless, in spite of such absurdity, the explanatory footnote to the verse in the Douay version reads 'That is, to the priest of the Church whom (verse 14) he had ordered to be called for and brought to the sick'. It is significant that the early Fathers of the Church never 'wrested' this passage of Scripture so as to make it give this impossible meaning. J. Bingham,[1] summing up the teaching of ancient writers in the early centuries on this subject, says: 'They advised all men, in case of lesser sins, to make confession mutually to one another, that they might have each other's prayers and assistance. This is the advice of St. James, v. 16.' Bingham then goes on to refer to a very interesting passage in one of Augustine's tractates on St. John, in which he expounds this verse of James in the light of the Saviour's words, 'If I, your Lord and Master, have washed your feet; ye also ought to wash one another's feet' (Jn. xiii. 14). 'Can we say', asks Augustine, 'that one brother may cleanse another from the contagion of sin? Yes, we are taught to do it by the mystical meaning of this work of our Lord, that we should confess our sins one to another, and pray one for another, as Christ intercedes for us. Let us hear St. James the apostle, evidently commanding this very thing, and saying, "Confess your faults one to another, and pray for one another", because in this our Lord hath set us an example. For, if He, who neither has, nor ever had, nor ever will have any sin, prays for our sins, how much rather ought we to pray for the sins of one another! And, if He forgive us, who has nothing to be forgiven by us, how much more ought we to forgive one another, who cannot live here without sin! Let us therefore forgive one another, and pray for each other's sins, that so we may in some measure wash one another's feet.'

It has already been suggested that the reference to healing in the words '*that ye may be healed*' should probably be regarded figuratively of spiritual, and not merely physical blessings, as in the reference to Is. liii. 5 in 1 Pet. ii. 24, 'by whose stripes ye were healed', and in the reference to Is. vi. 10 in Acts xxviii.

[1] *The Antiquities of the Christian Church*, XVIII, iii, 5.

27; Jn. xii. 40; and Mt. xiii. 15, 'and I should heal them'.

The main object of the confession of sins here advocated by James is not only that Christians may have mutual counsel, sympathy and comfort, but also the evoking of the great power of intercessory prayer, which only brethren who are reconciled to one another can offer with fervour and sincerity. He assumes that his readers know that God does not hear the ungodly, and that they will be careful only to make confession to fellow Christians, whether elders or others, who may be far from morally perfect, but who are justified sinners bound together by that indissoluble tie which unites all who have stood together at the foot of the Cross. In order to encourage them to make such confession to one another and to pray for one another, he recalls to their remembrance the great power of prayer as exemplified by the men of the Old Testament to whom the Jews did not hesitate to give the ascription *righteous*. Abel is so designated both by the author of the Epistle to the Hebrews (Heb. xi. 4) and also by Jesus Himself (Mt. xxiii. 35); and Lot is similarly described in 2 Pet. ii. 7.

The effectual fervent prayer of such men, as we can see from what is told us about them in the Old Testament, *availeth much.* There has been a good deal of rather profitless debate among scholars as to whether the present participle of the verb here used and translated *effectual fervent* (*energoumenē*) should be construed in the passive voice with some such meaning as 'prayer when it is exerted', or in the middle voice, as in the R.V. rendering, 'prayer in its working'. It is, in effect, very difficult to separate the two meanings. 'The same form', says J. H. Moulton,[1] 'can be used indifferently as active or passive in meaning'; and he draws attention to a similar ambiguity which exists in the English language in such expressions as 'he who hides (Active) finds' and 'he who hides (Passive) is secure'. This expression has, however, always been found somewhat tantalizing by translators. An old Latin manuscript translates it here by *frequens*, which is not an accurate rendering of the Greek, while the Latin Vulgate preferred *assidua*, 'persistent'. It was due to the influence of the Vulgate that Wycliffe trans-

[1] *Grammar of New Testament Greek Prolegomena*, p. 156.

lated it 'continual'. Tyndale, and all other English translators prior to the A.V., gave the word the interpretation favoured by Luther, 'fervent'. The A.V. combined both these renderings in the somewhat redundant *effectual fervent.* The R.S.V. follows but strengthens the R.V., 'the prayer of a righteous man has great power in its effects'. Whatever translation we may adopt, the main point of the sentence is clear. A righteous man's prayers differ from the prayers of others by virtue of their earnestness and their fervency. They are, moreover, not hindered so much by a sense of unworthiness; their motive is more unsullied; and, not least, they are controlled by a clearer understanding of what the righteous God demands. A man who walks uprightly with God cannot fail to pray in a manner acceptable to Him. His prayers must be efficacious.

James draws attention in the following verse to one outstanding instance of the efficacy of a righteous man's prayer. But many other illustrations could be given. A most interesting verse in this connection is Je. xv. 1, where God tells the prophet that His temporary rejection of His people is inevitable, and adds 'though Moses and Samuel stood before me, yet my mind could not be toward this people'. Moses and Samuel are obviously instanced as conspicuous examples of righteous men, whose prayers normally would be acceptable to God. The intervention of Moses on behalf of God's people, when 'his anger was kindled; and the fire of the Lord burned among them' during the journey to the promised land, certainly availed much; for 'when Moses prayed unto the Lord, the fire was quenched' (Nu. xi. 1, 2). In the same way, Samuel, at the time when the Israelites had shown disloyalty to their God by asking for an earthly king, called upon the Lord during the wheat harvest to send thunder and rain that the people might see that their wickedness was great. His sense of righteousness was in keeping with the righteousness of God, and the Lord sent the thunder and rain with the result that all the people greatly feared the Lord and Samuel. Later, when the people asked Samuel to pray further that they should not die, and made confession of their sin, he knew that such a prayer would be fully in harmony with the divine purpose, for God would never utterly forsake His people, and he said 'God forbid that I should sin against the Lord in ceasing to pray for you' (see 1 Sa. xii. 16–25). Other effective prayers of righteous men were Hezekiah's prayer that God would save the people from destruction at the hands of the Assyrian king Sennacherib (2 Ki. xix. 14–19), and the prayers of the same monarch who, more than almost any other king of Judah, did that which was right in the sight of the Lord, for his own recovery from illness (2 Ki. xx. 2–7).

17. If we ask why James should have chosen *Elias* as his sole illustration of the efficacious prayer of a righteous man, the answer would seem to be that Elijah had come to occupy in Jewish thought a unique position among the characters of the Old Testament. He was regarded as the prototype of the prophet who would immediately prepare the way for the coming of the Messiah; and it is as a second Elijah that John the Baptist is portrayed in the New Testament (see the description of John in Mk. i. 6, and our Lord's reference to him in Mk. ix. 13). As the earliest of the great prophets of Israel his name had become representative of the entire prophetic revelation, just as Moses was representative of the revelation embodied in the sacred law. It is, accordingly, Moses and Elijah who are found conversing with Jesus on the mount of Transfiguration (Mk. ix. 4). The fact, moreover, that Elijah had been translated direct to heaven without passing through the normal channel of death had greatly impressed itself upon the imagination of the Jewish people. It is not, in consequence, so surprising as it otherwise might seem to be that, when Jesus cried 'Eli, Eli' on the cross, some of those who stood near thought that He was calling upon Elijah in heaven to come down and save Him (Mk. xv. 34). The terrible drought, news of the beginning and of the end of which Elijah was commanded by God to convey to King Ahab (1 Ki. xvii. 1, xviii. 1), was always associated with his name. The praises of Elijah's achievements are fully sung by the author of Ecclesiasticus in the following eloquent passage, probably well known to James.

'Also there arose Elijah the prophet as fire,
Who brought a famine upon them,
And by his zeal made them few in number.
By the word of the Lord he shut up the heaven:
Thrice did he thus bring down fire.
How wast thou glorified, O Elijah, in thy wondrous deeds!
And who shall glory like unto thee?
Who did raise up a dead man from death,
And from the place of the dead, by the word of the Most
High:
Who brought down kings to destruction,
And honourable men from their bed:
Who heard rebuke in Sinai,
And judgements of vengeance in Horeb:
Who anointed kings for retribution,
And prophets to succeed after him:
Who was taken up in a tempest of fire,
In a chariot of fiery horses.'

(Ecclus. xlviii. 1–9, R.V.)

So wonderful did the achievements of Elijah seem to succeeding generations that he came to be regarded as semi-divine. Had he really been a superman his example would have been profitless to ordinary Christians. James accordingly is at pains to reassure his readers that the saints of the old covenant were no demi-gods. On the contrary, Elijah *was a man subject to like passions as we are.* The distinctive Greek word used here means literally 'suffering the same things', *homoiopathēs*, i.e. inheriting the same nature, subject to the same emotions, and liable to the same weaknesses. *Passions* perhaps narrows the meaning too much; and the rendering of the R.S.V., following R.V. margin, 'of like nature with ourselves' is preferable. The word is also found in Acts xiv. 15 where Paul is expostulating with the natives of Lystra who are on the point of offering sacrifice to himself and Barnabas as gods come down in the likeness of men. 'We also', he says, 'are men, of like nature with you' (R.S.V.). Similarly Peter had to restrain Cornelius from worshipping him by the reminder 'I myself also am a man' (Acts x. 26).

The sacred record of the story of Elijah in the first book of Kings, while it emphasizes the magnitude of his achievements, also draws attention to the ups-and-downs of his very human character. We find him alternating between the two extremes of buoyant confidence and of a self-distrust almost akin to despair. The Elijah whom we see in his ascendancy on Mount Carmel and the Elijah who confronts us in his despondency on Mount Horeb are strangely contrasted. He was indeed 'of like nature with ourselves'.

The statement in this verse that Elijah *prayed earnestly that it might not rain* is a natural deduction from the words of 1 Ki. xvii. 1 'the Lord God of Israel before whom I stand'; and the reference to the earnestness of his prayer on this occasion is an assumption, made perhaps in the light of the fervency of his prayer on Carmel when 'he cast himself down upon the earth, and put his face between his knees' (1 Ki. xviii. 42). The A.V. margin substitutes 'in his prayer' for *earnestly*, giving a literal rendering of the Greek. *Earnestly* is, however, almost certainly the right rendering of the Semitic idiom 'with prayer he prayed' which means 'he prayed intensely', just as the similar expression rendered in Lk. xxii. 15, 'With desire I have desired' means in fact 'I have heartily desired', the translation found in A.V. margin.

The reference to the length of the drought as the space of *three years and six months* would also appear to be a deduction from the text of 1 Ki. xviii. 1, where we read that 'after many days' the word of the Lord came to Elijah 'in the third year' bidding him to convey to Ahab news of the pending cessation of the drought. That this inference was not drawn for the first time by James is evident from the fact that our Lord in His reference to the same event in His address in the synagogue at Nazareth also spoke of the duration of the drought as 'three years and six months' (Lk. iv. 25).

18. It is here further assumed that the message Elijah received from God relating to the end of the drought (1 Ki. xviii. 1) came to him as an answer to prayer. The Old Testament narrative goes on to tell us that, when Elijah heard the first sound of the fall of rain, he prostrated himself on the mountain top before this manifestation of the sovereignty of God (1 Ki. xviii. 42). When James says that *the heaven gave rain* 'heaven' is in this context a synonym for 'God'. In 1 Ki. xviii. 1, God asserts that He will send rain upon the earth. Once the supernatural gift of rain is given, the earth, it is assumed, will inevitably bring forth her fruit. The association of rain and the products of nature is axiomatic in the Bible, as in Acts xiv. 17 'he did good, and gave us rain from heaven, and fruitful seasons'.

e. Reclaiming the backslider (v. 19, 20)

19. The connection between the last two verses of the Epistle and the previous section is not very clear, but it would seem to lie in the emphasis laid by the author on the privilege and duty of prayer in all circumstances. The brother who has wandered away *from the truth*, forgetting the great doctrines of the Christian faith which he embraced at his conversion, and unmindful of those ideals of moral conduct based upon them, must always be a primary concern of the other members of the fellowship to which he belongs. No duty laid upon Christians is more in keeping with the mind of their Lord, or more expressive of Christian love, than the duty of reclaiming the backslider; and it is very certain that such a work cannot be accomplished except by prayer and personal effort. So important is this aspect of their life as Christians that James, in stressing it, prefaces his words with an earnest and tender appeal to his readers contained in the address *Brethren*, or as the ancient MSS., followed by the R.V., read 'My brethren'. The general expression *one convert him* also makes it clear that this duty does not belong only to the elders, or to those who hold special office in the Church, but should be the concern of all.

For *one convert him* the R.S.V. has 'one brings him back', which is preferable. It is assumed that the erring brother is a converted Christian, and that he has only temporarily left 'the narrow way which leadeth unto life', and has to be brought back by personal contact from 'the broad way that leadeth to destruction' into the way of truth. It is not asserted that he is spiritually dead or is going to die, but that he is in a dangerous condition. The word *convert*, *epistrephō*, used here transitively, has an interesting parallel in Lk. xxii. 32, where it is used intransitively. Our Lord is there assuring the backsliding Simon Peter that He has prayed for him that his 'faith fail not', and says to him 'when thou art converted (R.S.V. 'when you have turned again') strengthen thy brethren'.

20. If the reading *Let him know* is followed, as it probably should be, James, in this closing verse of the Epistle, assures the particular Christian, who may be the means of reclaiming the backslider from *the error of his way*, how immense is the significance and how far-reaching are the consequences of the work he has accomplished. The alternative reading, 'Know ye' or 'Ye know', is probably a later adaptation of the principal verb of the sentence to the address *Brethren*.

The *soul* that is saved from deadly peril by such rescue work is described in some MSS. as 'his soul'; and that reading, preferred by Westcott and Hort because of its presence in the fourth-century *Codex Vaticanus*, is followed in the R.S.V. It is, however, probably due to an accidental repetition of the previous 'his'. But whether we read 'a soul' or 'his soul', the reference must surely be to the soul of the reclaimed sinner and not to the soul of him who reclaims him. Similarly, the *multitude of sins* which are covered are the sins committed by him who has wandered from the truth and not the sins of him who brings him back to the truth. It is very strange that Christian commentators should ever have thought that, in either of these last two clauses of the Epistle, James is advocating the recall of the backslider on the ground of the benefits it confers upon him who is responsible for it, rather than of the blessings achieved for the reclaimed sinner. Moffatt, for example, is quite certain whose sins are covered. 'Plainly', he wrote, 'the sins of the Christian who does the saving work. It is a popular way of saying, "That will atone for a good deal" . . . the brotherly love which is keen and true, charged with an intense sense of personal responsibility for the erring, as it flows from him to Christ, may be regarded as a kind of secondary atonement.'[1] It can no doubt be said with reference to all Christian acts of love, in the words of Elizabeth Browning, 'thou shall be served thyself by every sense of service that thou renderest'; but the view that salvation can be merited, forgiveness won and atonement achieved by such works, however charitable, though it is in keeping with Pharisaic Judaism, is wholly alien to New Testament Christianity, and to what James has said in i. 21. And unless we are to suppose that the Epistle of James is in fact not a Christian document at all, but a Jewish book which has somehow or other strayed in amongst the books of the New Covenant, this interpretation must be rejected. It is true that we read in Pr. x. 12, 'Hatred stirreth up strifes: but love covereth all sins', but the 'covering' there mentioned refers to the eagerness of love not to expose or gloat over the exposure of the sins of others. Such a thought is not pertinent to our present context, where the reference, as in 1 Pet. iv. 8, is to the covering of sins from God's sight so that they are forgiven.

It is sometimes urged that the clause *shall hide a multitude of sins* comes as an anticlimax after *shall save a soul from death*, if the reference in each case is to the sinner turned back from the error of his way; but, as Knowling well remarked, 'this is to ignore the truth that the soul is . . . not merely rescued from peril, but blessed'. The covering of sins so that they are hidden from God's sight is regarded in the Bible as supreme blessedness. 'Blessed is he', cries the Psalmist, 'whose transgression is forgiven, whose sin is covered' (Ps. xxxii. 1); and such blessing, as Paul makes very clear in the Epistle to the Romans, is the result of God's grace and is no human achievement. That God can and does 'cover' men's sins by treating them as though they had never been, and that the Christian who recalls the backsliding believer to the way of truth is being used to further the divine purpose of love, is thus the high note on which the Epistle ends. For all its apparent abruptness this ending is wonderfully arresting; it sounds a call in the ears of Christian men and women which they ought most carefully to heed, and to which they should be most eager to respond.

[1] *Love in the New Testament*, pp. 240, 241.